The Story of Early Mono County

ITS SETTLERS · GOLD RUSHES

INDIANS · GHOST TOWNS

Ella M. Cain

FEARON PUBLISHERS, INC.
SAN FRANCISCO, CALIF.

Foreword

This writing has been a work of love and inspiration. On reading it, now that it is finished, I realize that into its pages I have written an intimate part of my own life—a life spent on the scenes described in the book.

The lure and love of the mining camps are in my blood; they are an integral part of my lineage from pioneer ancestors.

My maternal grandparents, who lived in Hartford, Connecticut, answered the faraway cry of the gold rush to California in 1855. They came by way of Panama, riding on mule back across the Isthmus, then by sailing vessel to San Francisco. They joined the hundreds pouring into what was called the Northern Mines of California. My mother, Catherine Shaughnessy, was born in the little mining camp of Howland Flat, Sierra County, in 1862. Her family later moved to Virginia City, Nevada, and opened a hotel which burned in the big fire there on October 26, 1875.

In 1879, the family joined the thousands going into Bodie in the biggest gold rush known in years. Here my mother met and married M. J. Cody, the first Land Office Receiver in this part of the West. I was born in Bodie in 1882.

My father, on being elected Sheriff of Mono County in 1888, moved our family to the County Seat at Bridgeport. Here, I spent the most impressionable years of my life from six to fourteen.

After being sent away to school for some years, I came back to Bodie to teach. In 1904, I married David Victor Cain, son of the J. S. Cains, Bodie pioneers.

From thereon, I spent the greater part of my life in Bodie, that wild, exciting mining camp "on the top of the world."

During the last mining boom in Aurora, Nevada, from 1913 to

1917, my husband and I and our two little daughters, Helen and Ruth, moved to Aurora to take care of the Cain interests there. After these four years, we again returned to Bodie.

In giving you my own background, dear reader, I have intended to show the first hand knowledge I have of the places about which I have written. My hope is that I have conveyed this knowledge to you in an accurate and interesting way.

Having been intensely interested in the Piute Indian Tribe of Mono County, I have told much about them. I feel that writers of ethnology have not given the Piute Tribe their proper recognition. As a collector of Piute Indian baskets for over forty years, I had close contact with the Piutes of this region. This gave me an insight into their lives, customs, and traditions, which I hope this writing will preserve.

This book cannot be classed as a history, in the true sense of the word. I have purposely avoided controversial explorations, growth, and statistics crowded with figures.

I have also tried to confine the information to events that happened before the turn of the century.

While I have done a reasonable amount of research, there is no end of a chapter bristling with authorities and references. These were given, where they seemed to be needed, as the subject matter was written.

Instead, you will read about these intrepid souls, the *pioneers*, who settled here, and who suffered and braved the hardships of the frontier to lay the foundation of the Mono County we have today.

In closing, I wish to thank these friends who have kindly helped me in various ways towards making this book a success: Frashers of Pomona for permission to use many pictures; Lucy Harriett Whitney for permission to use the memoirs of her father, William Whitney, and letters of her uncle, G. A. Whitney, on early Bridgeport; all those who allowed pictures of their homes to be printed; Grace Kirkwood for the picture of Ah Quong Tai; Gilbert Wedertz for history of the Wedertz family; Miss Alice Dolan for numerous photos, newspaper clippings, and data on early Bridgeport; Cap Young for photo of Kirkwood homes; Sim Lundy for the account of the Indian Peace Treaty; Sarah Dick Gracian for information on the food of Piutes; the late Corde C. Hayes for photo of the second Courthouse; Celia Crocker Thompson for a photo of Bennettville; Mono County Clerk George Delury for co-operation in searching early county records; Maude Cohen for identifying people in group photos; the Stanley Hunewills for an early photo of the Hunewill ranch house; Mrs. Ruth Laughlin, Assessor, for help on early location; Mr. and Mrs. E. W. Billeb for photos; Oliver J. Kirkpatrick for a letter and information on Lundy; Margaret Calhoun for names of early Mono Lake settlers; Venita R. McPherson for data on Mono Lake Islands; Grace Bond for picture of Sam Fales; Doris Folsom for information on early Masonic, and for research on Jedediah Strong Smith; the late D. W. Hays, Engineer of Medicine Hat, Alberta, Canada, for a letter giving some important facts supplied in Ah Tai story; Mr. and Mrs. Harford Hays for help on identifying persons in group photos; Douglas Hubbard for information on Bennettville; my own dear mother who saved many early day newspapers, letters, and clippings, and my typists Mrs. Claire Hill and Mrs. Ethel G. Conley.

ELLA. M. CAIN

Contents

CHAPTER ONE

Early Explorations

The first explorations and entries into Mono County will be touched upon very lightly since historians like Bancroft, Farquhar, and others who have made an extensive study of the subject, differ as to the routes taken in California by the early explorers.

Francis P. Farquhar states that in the Spring of 1827, Jedediah Strong Smith, a fur trapper, and a party of men who had come up through California on the Western side of the Sierra Nevada, came down the eastern slope at Ebbets Pass. They crossed two northern flowing rivers, which appear to have been the east fork of the Carson River and the west fork of the Walker River.

Following the latter river, Smith rounded the south shore of Walker Lake and then traversed what he reported to be "The Great Sand Plain of Central Nevada."

Thus, a fur trapper in the year 1827 was the first *white* man to invade the sanctuary of the Piute Indians of the Mono region.

Robert Glass Cleland, in his *"History of California,"* states: "The first entry into Mono from the East was made in 1833 by Joseph Reddeford Walker, the frontiersman. This was an exploring and trapping party organized by Captain B. L. Bonneville of the U. S. Army as his own private venture. Walker, as leader of 40 horsemen, was instructed by Bonneville to cross the desert west of Salt Lake and proceed to California." It is generally agreed that he followed one of the tributaries of the Walker River, which bears his name, and crossed the mountains via what was later known as the Mono Trail.

John C. Fremont, the "Pathfinder," and his party, bent on exploration and acquisition of territory, crossed through western Nevada in the vicinity of Bridgeport in the winter of 1844. He had as his guide Kit Carson. Somewhere in the eastern ascent of the Sierra Nevada, presumably in the neighborhood above Leavitt Meadows, he had to abandon his 12 pound brass howitzer which, apparently, never has been found. Fremont Lake lies in the vicinity of his hazardous trail across the mountains.

In 1853, LeRoy Vining, a miner from Mariposa, hired an Indian guide to accompany him and his party to a gulch where gold had been found the preceeding year by Lieutenant Tredwell Moore of the United States Army. It is thought that Moore found the gold near Monoville. However, Vining settled in a meadow floor where he prospected for gold. This meadow was later called Lee Vining Canyon, in which the Tioga Pass Highway rises to a height of 2,000 feet. The town of Lee Vining near the west shore of Mono Lake was named in LeRoy Vining's honor.

CHAPTER TWO

The Naming of "Mono"

The Piute Indians, children of nature, living mostly in the open, and recognizing in our lofty peaks, rushing streams, topaz lakes, and vast forests all the beauties of nature, called this particular region *Mono* which meant in their language "beautiful."

The Indians, living across the Sierra Nevada Mountains on the western slope, who were known, after the coming of the white men, as Miwoks or "Diggers," called this whole region *Taboose*; *Taboose* means the land where grew a tuber at whose roots were clusters of soft, white nuts—mealy, milky, and sweet in taste (desired and bartered by all the tribes).

Hence the name Mono and Taboose—THE BEAUTIFUL—LAND OF THE SWEET GRASS ROOT.

CHAPTER THREE

Dogtown

Seven miles south of Bridgeport, on Highway 395, just above the Bodie road turn off, evidences can still be seen of extensive placer operations.

In 1857, Mormons in Nevada heard that a young German from Hanover named Cord Norst, with the pretty Indian girl he had taken as his wife, were panning out considerable placer gold, from what Norst had named "Dogtown Creek."

By 1859, about seventy or more Mormons had moved to Dogtown and had found panning and placering for gold a profitable venture.

A store with a goodly supply of groceries and liquors was owned and operated by a man named Loose. On July 4, 1859, a celebration was staged in the Loose establishment. A hot time was being had at old Dogtown. One of the celebrants called Chris decided to leave the party for some mysterious reason and wandered off over the hills. Could it be that John Barleycorn was being lured away by Lady Luck? After having gone several miles, Cord Norst related later, Chris lay on the ground to rest. Being a prospector at heart, he picked up some samples of the dirt around him. He rubbed his eyes— No! he couldn't be right! He was just seeing things! Just imagining his dream had come true! No, it *was* there, *GOLD*, precious *GOLD*, in no small quantity. He filled his pockets with the dirt and excitedly started back to Dogtown.

It was late afternoon by this time, and the party was still going strong, too strong, when he bolted in. The "boys" hooted and hollered when he showed them the dirt sparkling with gold. "Just a nice little trick," they said, "to break up a good party." Of course, he had "salted" the sample, just sprinkled a little of yesterday's pannings in the dirt to make suckers of them. No, they didn't intend to bite! Then

All that is left of Dogtown, scene of the first gold rush east of the Sierra Nevada

one of them, the worse for liquor than the rest, got up on a stool and decided they had better *hang* Chris for being a *liar* on the Fourth of July. Another across the room took a stool and told them Chris had always *been* an honest fellow, and *maybe* he *was* telling the truth. He would go back over the hills with Chris and prove it. Thereupon, they all decided to go, and a stampede started for the new gold discovery—and so MONOVILLE was born—the offspring of John Barleycorn and Lady Luck.

Dogtown was almost deserted, except for Cord Norst and his wife, who stayed there to placer gold in the sluice boxes of Dog Creek. They lived in a dug-out in the hill, the doors of which can still be seen on the hillside.

Later, others came to placer and pan for gold. The creek was lined in summer with bright red patches made by the calico dresses of the Indian women who were intent on shaking their pans and looking for that bright yellow line that formed around the edge.

The gold dust was brought to Bridgeport and weighed and sold at the Dave Hays store for many long years by Norst, his wife Mary, and many others.

CHAPTER FOUR

Monoville

Gold is a magic word!

Even in the days of practically no communications, the news of a new gold find spread like wildfire and rapidly reached the outside world.

Word that the precious particles could be picked right off the surface of the ground in Monoville and that every miner there was panning not less than one hundred dollars a day caused a stampede for the new excitement. The gold seekers came over the arduous trail, that has since become known as the Sonora Pass, from Jim Town, Sonora, Columbia, Chinese Camp, and all points of The Mother Lode to cast their lots in this new camp on the other side of the Sierra Nevada.

In a short time, Monoville had a population of 700 and all ground was soon claimed as far as Mono Lake—the Dogtowners of course getting the most promising claims.

Cord Norst of Dogtown, the authority for the story of the discovery of Monoville, also stated that all the men held back until Chris, the Discoverer, had located the ground he wanted. From there on, all track of Chris is lost.

Lumber being scarce in these parts, the miners first built log cabins or lived in dug-outs in the hillside. Later on, some large saws were brought and lumber was obtained from numerous timber belts in the mountains.

Soon, by common consent and a pooling of funds, a ditch was dug from what is now known as Virginia Creek to Monoville, and rockers and hydraulic operations were developed.

James Sinnamon was the most successful in working his claim. It lay along the side of the mountain over which the creek passed and from his claim he took $50,000 worth of gold. The old "Sinnamon Cut" can still be seen, like a red scar across the mountain, beyond the site where the Town of Monoville once stood. (Later, James Sinnamon took up ranching in Bridgeport Valley.)

By the Fall of 1859, disappointment at not becoming rich, inclement weather, and poor living conditions caused something of a general exodus of the red-shirted miners and their families. Only about 150 of the most courageous remained. Little did they know that they were facing one of the worst winters of that rugged country, and that starvation with her gaunt hands would threaten them.

By November 10th, five feet of snow covered the region. The remaining families had no communication with the outside world, no roads, not even trails, only deep, deep snow in every direction.

A meeting was called and it was decided that the nearest point where they could expect to get food was Genoa, Nevada, the Mormon Settlement in Carson Valley, a distance of over a hundred miles. Several of the strongest and bravest volunteered to go there on homemade "snow shoes."

Great was the rejoicing in Monoville when, after two weeks, they returned pulling on sleds behind them the desperately needed food. Had these brave men perished in the snow and not returned, the inhabitants of Monoville could not have survived a fate no less tragic than that which overtook the Donner party. In that case, Monoville would have gone down in California history as a landmark where happened one of the greatest tragedies of our California pioneer days. Instead it has sunk into oblivion.

Mark Twain immortalized the camp to some extent in "Roughing It," where he spoke of the Monoville region as having two seasons: "The breaking up of one winter, and the beginning of the next."

And further in respect to the weather, Twain wrote:

"Under favorable circumstances, it snows at least once in every single month in the year, in the little town of Mono. So uncertain is the climate in summer that a lady who goes out visiting cannot hope to be prepared for all emergencies unless she takes her fan under one arm and her snowshoes under the other. When they have a Fourth of July procession, it generally snows on them, and they do say that as a general thing when a man calls for a brandy toddy there, the barkeeper chops it off with a hatchet and wraps it up in a paper, like maple sugar."

Much more gold was taken out of Monoville, and the surrounding area known as Mono Diggings, than will ever be accounted for, as it was worked not by companies but by the owners of the claims themselves.

In 1864, when the County Seat of Mono County was found to be in Nevada and had to be moved into California, a choice was given to the people between Monoville and Bridgeport. Bridgeport was chosen as it seemed to have more permanency, which proved to be correct.

Monoville went on for many years, but the population dwindled as new camps like Aurora and Bodie came into prominence.

The discoverer of Bodie, William Bodey, lost his life in a snow storm in 1859 while trying, with his partner Black Taylor, to take supplies to Bodie from Monoville.

The Rattle Snake Mine at Monoville, having a fair ledge, was purchased and developed in the early 1890's by the writer's father, M. J. Cody.

A shaft was sunk about 200 feet deep and a tunnel was run which produced some rich ore. Water came into the shaft to such an extent that after two pumps were found to be inadequate, work in the shaft had to be given up. About fifteen men worked there for over two years. The "clean up" was made in an arastra.

When my father used to ask the "Cousin Jack" (Cornish) foreman, Harry Trevathen, how good the ledge was looking, Harry would give one of two answers: "She's pointin' toward the boardin' house, Mister," meaning "good," or, again; "She's pointin' toward the poor house, Mister." But it pointed too often towards the "poor house" and the work was finally discontinued.

A man still having faith in the Monoville region is J. Cap Young. He is developing properties below the site of Monoville.

Monoville was like a "flash in the pan" in California gold rush history, but it can always claim the honor of being the first of the gold camps east of the Sierra Nevada Mountains. And further, if some of the early historians are correct, *it was the first place* where gold *was discovered* in California by Trapper Jedediah Smith and his men who found gold near or in Monoville in the late 1820's and took the samples back to Salt Lake City, Utah.

CHAPTER FIVE

Early Mono County

Mono County was created on April 24th, 1861, by an act of the California Legislature. It was one of the first mining counties to be organized east of the Sierra Nevada Mountains. Located in the east central part of California, Mono County is about 150 miles in length and 50 miles in width.

In its first nine years, the County suffered three major setbacks by losing much territory. The first one was in 1863 when the boundary line was changed between Nevada and California, giving Aurora, the then County Seat of Mono County, to Esmeralda County, Nevada. The second occurred in 1866 when the southern part of Mono County was detached to form part of Inyo County. In 1870, when the Legislature defined the boundary of Inyo County as being 20 miles further north, another chunk of territory was taken from Mono County and added to Inyo County. The latter agreed to pay Mono $12,000 for the transfer. This, Inyo County eventually did.

The first County Elections were held June 6, 1861, the County Seat, at that time, being Aurora.

The officers elected were:

R. M. Wilson—County Clerk	William Feast—Treasurer
N. F. Scott—Sheriff	L. Tuttle—Surveyor

The first Supervisors were E. Green, C. P. Woodland, and J. S. Schultz. They held their first meeting in Aurora on June 13, 1861. (Bancroft, *California Vol. XXV,* P. 163)

The Governor of California appointed as Judge, J. A. Moultric, who resigned shortly afterward and was replaced by Judge Baldwin. (Sheriff Scott was killed by the Indians and G. W. Bailey was appointed to fill the vacancy.)

Courthouse in Aurora when it was the County Seat of Mono County

Soon after the first election, a most disturbing situation arose for Mono County: The Territory of Nevada had been organized by an Act of Congress on March 2nd, 1861, (about seven weeks before the creation of Mono County) and President Lincoln appointed James W. Nye Territorial Governor of Nevada. Nye, four months after his appointment, issued a proclamation for an election of members of The Territorial Council and House of Representatives and included Aurora as one of the districts in Esmeralda County, Nevada. This lead to a heated dispute as to the boundary line between California and Nevada.

A small civil war, often referred to as "The Sagebrush War," was already in progress north of Lake Tahoe, between Roop County, Nevada and Plumas County, California over the boundary line in Honey Lake Valley. Commissioners were named jointly by the State of California and the Territory of Nevada to define the line by making a survey. But before the survey was completed at Lake Tahoe, Governor Nye named a set of officers for Esmeralda County, Nevada, and Chief Justice Turner of Nevada opened court in Aurora, Esmeralda County, Nevada. Judge Baldwin of Mono County meanwhile continued to sit on the bench maintaining he was in Aurora, *Mono County, California.*

In the September elections of 1863, with the survey of the boundary *still* unfinished, elections were held for both counties. Two sets of officers were elected, one set for Mono County and one set for Esmeralda County. The Aurorans treated the balloting as a hilarious "Hell bent for Election" occasion, as they were privileged to vote at the two voting places, if they so chose——at Armory Hall for the Esmeralda County officials and at the Police Station for the Mono County officials.

Union Republicans were elected on both tickets. At this Civil War time, there was much strife in Aurora as the Confederates had many sympathizers. Within twenty days after the election, the survey *was* completed and Aurora was found, according to the survey, to be three miles inside the Nevada line.

By the bend in the map at Lake Tahoe, California lost much territory; and disgruntled Californians contended that a jog had been placed in the line in order to give Nevada more territory and locate Aurora, which was then a thriving mining community of several thousand persons, inside the Nevada limits.

Some street and saloon fights took place, and early writers claim a duel was fought, but stories of violence and men "armed to the teeth" are much exaggerated.

It is interesting to note the different reactions of the Mono County officials on knowing for a certainty that Aurora was no longer the County Seat of Mono. Judge Baldwin closed his court at once and announced he would try no more cases there. Sheriff Teel (newly elected) resigned, remained in Aurora, and was appointed a Deputy Sheriff of Esmeralda County. County Clerk R. M. Wilson and Treasurer William Feast loaded some of the records into a wagon and took them across the line to Bodie where it was said the Mono officials had their offices under their hats.

Mono County's second Courthouse

Mono County called a special election in the Spring of 1864 for the voters to determine where the County Seat of Mono was to be in the future. Monoville, within sight of Mono Lake and a lively mining camp of several hundred people, and Bridgeport were the contenders for the honor.

Bridgeport won the election. The first meeting of the Supervisors held in the new County Seat was September 1, 1864. Esmeralda County ordered a transcript of the records made, but on receiving word that it would cost $10,000, dropped the matter.

John N. Dudleston, newly elected County Clerk, brought some of the records of his office to Kingsley's Inn on the east side of the river in Bridgeport, and the other officers took up their quarters there. Hence, this rambling one story building became Mono County's second Courthouse.

Later, A. F. Bryant, then Chairman of the Board of Supervisors,

Present day Mono County Courthouse

and J. W. Towle were appointed to bring the remaining records to the new County Seat. It took three trips by buck board and horses to get the records to Bridgeport.

In 1878-79, as money began to roll into the County Treasury at 6% (mostly on taxable property in Bodie), the Board of Supervisors decided that a new Courthouse should be built. On June 29, 1880, they accepted a bid of $22,900 submitted by the firm of Anton, Cain, and Hopkins to build the present Courthouse. However, this amount was found to be insufficient and the Bridgeport Chronicle-Union of March 26, 1881, states, "The Courthouse when finished cost $31,000." The foundation is of Bodie granite.

While this still-imposing building is now the second oldest Courthouse in California, it is admired for its stateliness and charm by the many thousands of people who vacation in Bridgeport, and those who travel Highway 395.

The cannon on the lawn was made in the Standard Machine Shop in Bodie and was presented to the County by J. S. Cain.

The citizens of Bridgeport had a real celebration on the completion of the Courthouse as stated in the Bridgeport Chronicle-Union of March 26, 1881:

"A procession was formed at twilight and marched from the old Courthouse to the new courtroom where the lawyers delivered humorous speeches and all had a gay time." Later on April 2, 1881, the Chronicle-Union notes that "Loose's Saloon is being moved uptown opposite the Leavitt House near the new Courthouse."

INDUSTRIES

The discoveries of gold and silver on the east side of the Sierra Nevada Mountains brought the mining industry into first importance. This was followed by the supplemental industries of stock and sheep raising, lumbering, dairying, and farming.

MINING

Around 1863 the mineral resources of Mono were being opened up. There was the new Montgomery District in southern Mono and, in 1865, the mines at Benton were causing some excitement. The change from placer to quartz mining also changed the status of independent miners to employees of mining companies.

In 1877 The Lake Mining District, 25 miles south of Mono Lake, was organized. Situated in the High Sierra, the district had 15 small lakes within a radius of 10 miles.

Then in 1879 came the Bodie boom and about the same year W. J. Lundy started mining on the May Lundy mine in the Homer Mining District.

The Great Sierra Consolidated Silver Mining Company started to develop the Tioga Mine at the head of Lee Vining Canyon about the year 1880. Bancroft states in *California Vol. XIX*, page 298: "In 1886 Mono County produced more gold and silver than any other County in California with the exception of Nevada County."

In its early history, Mono County had mining excitements, gold rushes, and boom camps. Now the latter can well be called "Ghost Towns of Mono."

With the exception of Bodie and Benton, they have all been leveled off, either by the elements or by being carried away timber by timber, brick by brick.

However, these once exciting boom camps of early California, where gun play was the rule instead of the exception, have left their interesting history to be recorded and appreciated by other generations; also, they have added materially to the wealth of California by the millions of dollars which they produced.

Later in this book, some writing will be devoted to some of these short-lived mining towns of Mono County, namely Dogtown, Monoville, Aurora, Bodie, Benton, Bennettville, Lundy, Tioga, Mammoth City, and Masonic.

FARMING

At an early date, Bridgeport Valley and Antelope Valley (Coleville) were opening up as the fertile districts in the County. The big broad acres of Bridgeport Valley were supplying many thousand cattle and sheep with pasturage. Much hay was cut and stored away for winter use.

Antelope Valley, while still pasturing stock, was more given to products such as apples, berries, pears, wheat, honey, etc., and much of this produce was sold in early Bridgeport.

At Mono Lake, farmers began to move in early and took up homesteads on the north, south, and west shores, where the land was well watered by numerous creeks of the High Sierra; but the eastern shore of the lake remained barren and uncultivated.

The Mammoth and Long Valley regions were settled early by the Summers and Magee families who saw the fine pasturage for cattle and sheep in these valleys.

LUMBER INDUSTRY

The demand for lumber around the early 60's caused a number of saw mills to be built around Big Meadows (Bridgeport). In 1866 the output from these steam driven saw mills totaled 400,000 feet of lumber and 330,000 shingles. (Above from Assembly & Senate Journal, 18th Session).

This lumber was mostly used in the construction of dwellings for Bridgeport, since the Bodie boom came later (1879). Thereafter, Bridgeport shipped much lumber to Bodie.

In 1881, the Bodie Railway & Lumber Company was organized

with Robert N. Graves as President. The lumber region to be tapped was about 7 miles south of Mono Lake and was later called Mono Mills.

Chinese labor was at first employed to construct the railroad. White labor in Bodie, especially the Miners Union, objected to the Chinese being hired and formed a delegation to go on foot to Mono Lake, a distance of 21 miles, to make a strong protest against the Chinese. Superintendent Holt had received advance notice of the coming of the "Bodieites" and had the Chinese taken by steamer and scow to the nearest island in Mono Lake. The lake has never again heard anything like the sing-song gibberage of these "chinks." When the tired Bodieites reached the spot where the Chinese had been camped, they found it vacant—even the water and supplies having been removed. The Chinese were discharged when the road was at a point within several miles of Bodie, and white labor was employed from that point on. In December of 1881, this railroad was finished. It had cost one million dollars.

In 1882, five million feet of lumber and twenty seven thousand cords of wood were hauled into Bodie from Mono Mills on this narrow gauge road. Four mogul type engines pulled the loaded flat cars. The engines were called The Mono, The Inyo, The Bodie, and The Tybo. The Mono, Inyo, and Bodie Engines were sold as junk along with the rails and equipment during World War I. The Tybo engine is now owned by Warner Brothers Pictures.

ROADS

The settlement of the Eastern slope was greatly retarded by lack of roads which were necessary for the growing activity of the region.

An Editorial in the Oakland Tribune of Sunday, January 18, 1948, under Knave Features, has this to state:

"In the winter of 1860, Dave Hays built a small cabin in Eureka Valley.

"James John Welch had his cabin at a spot known as Niagra.

"Major Lane was stationed at Strawberry.

"G. W. Brightman was established at Brightman's Flat.

"Hiram Leavitt was at Leavitt Meadows, and Sam Fales was proprietor at Fales Hot Springs.

"These were known as 'The Snow Shoe Men' and carried the mail from Sonora to Bridgeport."

The relatives of Dave Hays told the writer that Dave had his feet frozen on one of these trips and had to have several toes amputated, causing him to have a slight limp afterwards.

A stranger insisted, under protest, on going alone over the trail on a stormy day in winter when Sam Fales and Leavitt were not due to make connections. His body was found along the trail in the snow the following spring and buried by Hays, Welch, and Leavitt. The stream near where they buried him was called "Dead Man's River." Hays, Welch, and Leavitt later settled in Bridgeport.

The first wagon road was built over the Sierra Nevada Mountains in August 1856, and ran between Murphy's, California and Carson Valley.

This road necessitated a hundred miles of additional travel from Carson to get into the Mono region. By a bond issue of Mono County and the passage of a bill by the California Legislature in 1863, work was started from Sonora, Tuolumne County to Bridgeport, Mono County, in 1864. The road was completed in 1868. As the bond issue was exhausted and as our Assemblyman Joseph Wassen wrote, "It involved several Counties in deepest debt," a franchise was issued making it a toll road. The road had cost $400,000 and was closed by deep snows many months of the year.

Aurora and Monoville now being in the decline, many people wondered if the building of the Sonora road was warranted by the travel going over it. However, in 1879 when Bodie was at the height of its boom, the road was alive with traffic. The highways and byways were conjested with all sorts and manners of vehicles—stage coaches, twenty mule teams, pack teams, dead-ox wagons, lumber teams, fruit wagons from Tuolumne, weary prospectors trudging along beside heavily loaded burros, gamblers, prostitutes, buggies with speculators drawn by spirited horses—all bent on being the first to ply their trade in the new found gold camp "on the top of the world."

The wagon road which had served Aurora by stage coaches from Carson City was extended to Bodie about 1861, but regular stages did not come into the camp until several years later.

In 1879, the stage line from Carson to Bodie ran eight daily stages regularly with fifty-four horses stationed at each of nine stops.

SCHOOLS

Early data on schools seems to be very vague. Not many children were brought into this County during the gold rush excitements and the settlement of these outposts of civilization.

In 1861, when Aurora was the County Seat of Mono County, a brick school house was constructed by Mono County for the 80 children in Aurora. At this writing, December, 1959, this school house is about the only building left standing in Aurora.

In 1866, when Northern Owens Valley was still part of Mono County, the first teacher, Mrs. Joel Smith, taught a small group of children in her home. The school was maintained by private subscription.

In the early 1880's, a fine school house was built in Bodie on upper Green Street. It burned down a short time later. (Many people thought the fire was of incendiary origin.) The County then purchased the two story Bon Ton Lodging House, lower down on Green Street, and remodeled it into a school house. It is still standing.

Miss Alice M. Walker was one of Bridgeport's first teachers. She was a teacher in Sonora, Tuolumne County, California, before coming to Mono. She married David Hays of Bridgeport. She was the *first woman County* Superintendent of Schools in the State of California, serving from 1876 to January 1878. Years later, she again took up the duties of Superintendent of Schools of Mono County, and was a member of the Mono County Board of Education for forty years. Her daughter Cordelia Hays Dolan, also a teacher, was Superintendent of Schools of Mono County for twelve years.

In the 1890's, Mono County maintained a school at the Scanavino Ranch (then known as the Goat Ranch) at Mono Lake for the children of the Scanavino family *alone.* There were twelve of them. Nothing but Italian had been spoken in the home, so English had

Alice M. Walker, one of Bridgeport's first school teachers and the first woman County Superintendent of Schools in California

to be taught first. A girl named Mary Roux was hired to do this at a small salary and board, *paid by the County.* Many funny episodes ensued. A Mono Lake rancher was asked "How are you getting along, John. Are you making any money?" He shook his head disconsolately and answered "No—I no maka-th-mon. That Italian wop of a Joe Scanavino eata-the-mam-school maka-the-mon."

At one time a man whose wagon had broken down knocked on the Scanavino door. The door was opened slightly and a young head appeared. The man inquired, "Could I borrow a monkey wrench from you?" "No," said young Scanavino, "this no the monkey ranch, this the Goat Ranch."

However, the children proved to be very apt at learning. One of the boys named Steve became almost an electrical genius. By study-books, he constructed a small power plant on an irrigation ditch in back of the ranch house. It furnished electric lights for the ranch and turned off automatically, by clock, every night at 10. Steve afterward held many responsible positions with large electrical companies.

HYDRO ELECTRIC POWER

Mono County can claim the honor of having the first long distance power plant in existence. Up to 1892, though electric power had been developed, it had been used only at its source.

Tom Legett, the then Superintendent of the Standard Mine in Bodie, had a strong conviction that power could be transmitted by wires to any distance. After many meetings and discussions by the stockholders, he finally gained permission to erect an electric power plant at Green Creek, seven miles above Bridgeport; the power to be used to run the Standard Mill in Bodie, a distance of 13 miles. The Standard Company bought the site they needed from the then Land and Cattle Baron of Mono County, T. B. Rickey. Construction of a plant was immediately started.

It was called "Legett's Folly" and many of the stockholders thought the Company was throwing away its money.

The surveyors were instructed to have no angles or curves in the line in case the electricity would fly off into space. A telephone line was built parallel to the power line.

The Standard Mill was shut down and equipped with agitator motors, generators, and everything needed to change from steam to this "questionable" power. Again a hue and cry went up from the stockholders at the expense due to the shut down of the mill.

Tom Legett and his staff realized if this experiment turned out to be a failure, their reputations were ruined and their jobs gone.

At last all was in readiness for testing the "great experiment." A small crowd of very tense men stood in front of the switchboard in the Standard Mill. The switches on both ends were thrown in. Slowly the lights came on; dim at first, then brighter. The wheels of the small motor began to turn, the big motors started to vibrate; then came the joyful sound of a steady hum.

YES, electric power *could* be transmitted for a distance over wires. A more jubilant crowd of men could not be found anywhere. They hugged each other, threw their hats into the air, and shouted. Then someone broke a bottle of champagne over the first motor to turn by long distance power.

No word ever flashed around the world more quickly, and there was a scramble for power sites from Rhodesia to Australia.

Tom Legett was quickly hired by the English Government to build power plants in South Africa. All of the men connected with helping to build this little power plant on Green Creek, Mono County, were given important positions by the English Government.

The Green Creek plant developed 6600 volts and 350 electrical horse power.

James S. Cain, then one of the stockholders in the Standard Mine and later its owner, located two wonderful power sites in the higher Sierra Nevada Mountains in Mono. One was the Lee Vining site at the head of Silvester Meadows near the Tioga road, and the other was the Rush Creek site, at Silver Lake. Huge power plants were built on these sites by The Pacific Power Co., now known as California Electric Power Co. This power is being transmitted and used throughout Southern California as far as the Mexican border.

SCENIC WONDERS

Mono indeed is a land of great scenic beauty and the varied wonders of lakes, glaciers, rivers, trout streams, valleys, meadows, precip-

One of Mono County's numerous creeks

itous canyons, sagebrush covered areas, forests and mountain peaks. Three of the latter, Mt. Dana, Mt. Lyell, and Castle Peak rise to a height of about 13,000 feet. On many of its mountains can be seen perpetual snow.

Here is a list of some of Mono's scenic wonders worth visiting:

Devils Post Pile, Mammoth

Rainbow Falls, Mammoth

The Mammoth Minarets

Earthquake Fault, Mammoth

Petroglyphs (Ancient Indian writing on rocks), Birchim Canyon—Fish Slough

Balanced Rock at June Lake

Mono Lake with its Islands and Craters

The Crags above upper Twin Lakes, Bridgeport

Face looking up in the sky—Crags, Twin Lakes, Bridgeport

Travertine Deposit, Bridgeport

The topography of Mono County is generally rough and mountainous, especially along the eastern side, the back bone of the Sierra Nevada.

The County has three principal rivers, the two Walkers and the Owens, and numerous turbulent creeks cascading down its mountain sides and later flowing placidly along through green meadows.

The East and West Walker rivers which run through Mono's canyons miles apart are harassed by dams for irrigation projects in Nevada. These impounded rivers form two beautiful lakes, Bridgeport Lake on the east, and Topaz Lake on the west. The two Walker's join together in Nevada and supply water for an "inland sea," Walker Lake, near Hawthorne, Nevada.

The Owens river has its source in the east Mammoth region and it, and its tributaries, are impounded in Long Valley where they spread out to form beautiful Crowley Lake in whose bosom is reflected the giant peaks of the High Sierras. This lake is a major part of the metropolitan water system of Los Angeles, and the favorite fishing center for thousands of vacationers from the southland. It was named in honor of Father J. J. Crowley, "the Padre of the Desert," who lost his life in an auto accident near Lone Pine. Further on, the river from Crowley Lake is diverted into the Los Angeles aqueduct, which takes its God-given waters over deserts and mountains for hundreds of miles to refresh the southland with what was originally the melting snow of the High Sierras of Mono County.

CHAPTER SIX

Bridgeport

In the heart of its own vast empire, sparkling like a jewel at the foot of the High Sierras, lies Bridgeport, County Seat of Mono, fast becoming noted throughout the West for its great scenic beauty and for the recreational attractions of its lakes, rivers, and mountains.

The following chapters will tell of the pioneers who settled in this valley, and some of whose descendants still remain here to the fourth, fifth, and sixth generations.

Big Meadows was the name by which Bridgeport Valley was known for a number of years.

About 1855, farmers began to hear of the fertile acres of grass-covered virgin soil to be found east of the Sierra Nevada Mountains and eventually came from different parts of the United States to settle there. It had a background truly American. They found deer, game, and fish in abundance, so had no great problem as far as food was concerned.

Although the summers were mild and delightful, the winter climate was severe with below zero temperatures and deep snows.

One cannot help but reflect on the great courage and fortitude of these early pioneers who settled in a valley that overwhelmed them by its beauty, awed them by its vastness, and challenged them by its hardships.

The first white man to spend a winter in Big Meadows was George Byron Day (later known as "By" Day). "By" Day was followed shortly afterward by N. B. Hunewill, W. T. Elliott, the Whitney Brothers, J. Green, David Hays, J. W. Towle, James H. Patterson, Joseph W. Kingsley, the Huntoon Brothers, Sidney and Almond; Louis Ladd, Charles Stewart, A. F. Bryant, Dr. Clark

Sinclair, James Sinnamon, Andrew H. Allen, Hiram L. Leavitt, P. G. Hughes, Jesse Summers and others.

The first men to come to Big Meadows by wagon train were William Whitney, his brother G. A. Whitney, and a man named Green.

Miss Lucy Whitney of Cleveland, Ohio, has given me permission to quote from the written Memoirs of her father, Wm. Whitney of Bangor, Maine, who said of this experience: "We came at the invitation of a man named Green who had traveled with us across the plains. We ran the first wagon train that ever went up the East Walker River canyon; ten miles of terror in the River and over boulders, under water with a very swift current. We came into a valley as beautiful as Paradise with the purest water and richest grass I ever saw. Now our stock were happy and grew fat fast. We were surrounded by high mountains. We built a log house for Mr. Green on the east side of the valley, and we went over to the west side to locate a ranch for ourselves. My brother G. A. Whitney, was better, though he nearly bled to death from taking so much medicine to stop the ague."

The Whitney brothers took up by preemption a large acreage of ground which they later sold to a man named Coddington, who in turn sold it to "By" Day. It is still known as the By Day Ranch (from records on file in Bridgeport).

A note from G. A. Whitney to his brother William (presumably sent by carrier across the valley, as it was written on just a folded piece of paper) read thus:

No Date
(Probably 1862)

"Bro. William.........

We hear account of some Indian trouble at Huntoon's Ranch. I have sent some powder and caps for Perry, you had better keep your arms in good order and a good look out, and if there should be any threatening by all means let us know and several of us here will go out and see how the thing looks, and if need be give them "hail columbia" don't give up that pistol to anybody until Tinkham calls for it. There will probably be trouble with the Indians before the thing is over but they are so scattered that the whites can clean them in two weeks after they start in—Perry will give Jack Severe a sack of Flour as one will be coming to him if not more, after eatting, up to the time he goes away, and he will also give some pickles and bal of stuff coming to him— If you want a quarter of beef of Perry he will let you have it at 10cts and I will pay for it when Perry comes in—

G. A. Whitney"*

The Piute Indians were located mainly around the hot springs—Fales, The Big Hot, Travertine and Buckeye Canyon. They were shy, and usually retreated giving the white settlers very little trouble.

Sim Lundy, whose grandfather took part in a peace pact with the whites, is still living in Bridgeport. To this author, Sim gave the following account of the coming of the white man into the valley:

"Long time ago lots of Indians live in Bridgeport Valley called Big Meadows. Good hunting, good fishing then. When white men come with guns and Indians saw birds and animals getting killed they were heap afraid. They pick up everything and all go away into the mountains where white man could not find them. Always there were Indian scouts looking to see what white man was doing.

Then white man bring hog-a-di (food) and blanket not made of skins, where Indian could get them. When sometimes they saw Indian they would put down gun on ground so Indian would not be afraid.

After long time Captain Jim of Indians, talk to white man named By Day. Pretty hard talkem. By Day give him gun and tell him for all the Indians to come to place near Bridgeport, Big Hot, and bring bows and arrows. White man would bring guns and put them on ground in pile, Indians would put bows and arrows down in another pile. Then Indian would race white man, and first ones would pick up what he wanted. Indians beat white man in race and all Indians took guns. Then By Day put out his hand to Charlie Creek Indian, and more white man, West Towle, Bill Elliott, Dave Hays, Whitneys, and Hunewill, all put out hand to Indian. That's what

*Miss Lucy Whitney recently loaned to the Nevada Historical Society in Reno, for her life time, copies of her father's memoirs and the letters written by her uncle, G. A. Whitney, in Aurora, Mono County, California, and sent to his brother in Iowa.

my grandfather say, and they all shaked hand. White man say to Indian 'We friends now.' Then we all sit down and smoke peace-pipe, one pass it to next man till all men smoked. Then we all eat food of white man.*

White man showed Indian how to use gun. Most time Indian and white man had no trouble in Bridgeport Valley. But one time all white men came near being killed by Indians, when one Chinaman named Ah Tai made Indian eat Indian meat." (Referring to Ah Tai trouble).

The year 1863 brought a great drought to California and stockmen throughout the State began driving their cattle to the High Sierra country to save them from starvation. Big Meadows furnished abundant pasturage for many thousands of these cattle. Since that time, the custom of pasturing cattle in the Sierra for summer feeding is still in effect, although in the 80's and 90's much hay was cut and stored for winter feeding. (This was before the Bridgeport farmers had acquired ranches in Nevada.) In 1863, hay cut in Bridgeport sold readily in Aurora at $100.00 a ton.

The most urgent need of the early settlers in Big Meadows was for lumber. There was abundant timber in the surrounding mountains and several saw mills driven by steam were quickly built and put in operation. I. P. Yaney erected in the canyon a sawmill which bears his name today. The Twin Lakes mill was built by Z. B. Tinkum, the Robinson mill by George Robinson on Robinson creek. Two sawmills were built in Buckeye Canyon by N. B. Hunewill. (An old logging wagon with solid wooden wheels is still to be seen on the site of this logging camp. A tree has grown up through the middle part of it.)

(The first white women to live in what is now Bridgeport were Mrs. Vaughn and Mrs. Parsons, who were cooks at this Hunewill Sawmill.)

Oxen teams were used to do the hauling and many hundred oxen could often be seen grazing in the green meadows.

A blacksmith shop to shoe the oxen was one of the first frame

*William Whitney also tells in his memoirs of smoking the peace-pipe with the Indians.

Main Street, Bridgeport. Dave Hays' store at left and the Allen House (later Brandon House) at right

buildings to be built. This was erected just east of the footbridge on the East Walker River in 1863. As this shop was close to the road leading up the East Walker River Canyon, other buildings sprung up near it. Bryant and Reese started a store. Louis Ladd put up a hotel. Joseph W. Kingsley built an Inn, which was later used as the Courthouse on the removal of the County seat from Aurora. And this little settlement *across* the *bridge* came to be known as *Bridgeport.* So it was that the *name* of the County seat of Mono came into being.

With the output of lumber at the sawmills, new homes and buildings were built *west* of the bridge, and the townsite as it stands today was laid out. The principal street, called Main, runs East and West.

It must be said to the credit of those early carpenters, among them Peter Nye, Jesse McGath, Hiram L. Leavitt, Adam Kidd, Sam Hopkins, and Michael Whalen, that the structures they built were among the best to ever go up in Bridgeport, and have stood the test of time.

The J. W. Towle house, for which Joshua W. Towle, pioneer cabinet maker and treaty maker, himself sawed the lumber at the

J. N. Towle house, Bridgeport

"By" Day's house

N. B. Hunewill Ranch, now the popular Circle H

Leavitt House

The Dave Hays family on the porch of their store with the author second from left—site is now occupied by the Sierra Lodge Motel

The John Stewart home (left) and the Thomas Kirkwood home (right)

W. T. Elliott Ranch

W. P. Brandon's valuable black stallion, Cheri

Jess Summers' home- now owned by David Hays' granddaughter, Alice M. Dolan

Hunewill sawmill and helped to build in 1875, is still lived in by his granddaughter Miss Naomi V. Smith. The Towle family long served Mono as County officials.

The G. B. Day residence is still lived in by the fifth generation of Day's, whose occupations have always been farming.

The N. B. Hunewill ranch and home has been owned by the Hunewill family for six generations and is now the popular Circle H Guest Ranch. The Hunewell's will celebrate their centennial in 1961, the date of the first water right issued to N. B. Hunewill. Frank Hunewill, son of N. B. Hunewill, was Assemblyman from Mono-Inyo Counties in the early 1890's.

"WEDERTZ FAMILY"

In 1879, a family which was destined to play a large part in the development of the community moved to Bridgeport.

The father, Louis Wedertz, was born in Germany in 1825, the eleventh son in a family of fifteen children.

At the age of twenty-four, Louis determined to come to America to evade being drafted into the German Army. At the dock in Hanover, Germany, he stowed away in a dry-goods box. The box later dropped into the harbor and he narrowly escaped drowning; but by

Bridgeport Community Church

good luck, he landed in New Orleans where he met and married his wife Dorothy. Together they crossed the Isthmus of Panama on burros in 1853, coming first to San Francisco, then on to Sulphur Springs, Nevada, then to Aurora, and finally to the East Walker River where they took up a homestead in 1874.

Five years later, Louis moved his family of five daughters and three sons to Bridgeport. Here he started a store. The Wedertz daughters married prosperous and prominent men in the commu-

Sierra Cash Grocery

nity. The sons became business men. His son, Ed Wedertz, started the sheep raising industry in Mono County.

When Louis' son Frank decided to build a new home, the family gave their old home to the town of Bridgeport to be used as a Community Church. It was moved from near the river to its present site where, for years, it has served its good purpose.

It was a *long* road and perhaps a *hard* one that you traveled, Louis Wedertz, from a dry-goods box in the harbor of Hanover, Germany, to a faraway valley in California, where there stands a fitting monument to your life's work—a little white church in the High Sierras. (The three young daughters of our present District Attorney and Mrs. Denton, are, on the mother's side, the sixth generation of the Wedertz family still living in Bridgeport.)

A man who did much for early Bridgeport was A. F. Bryant, who founded the firm of Bryant & Reese across the bridge. This store he later moved uptown. It is still owned by the fourth generation of Bryants and known as the Sierra Cash Grocery.

A. F. Bryant's ranch comprised most of the land where the Town of Bridgeport now stands. He gave *outright* to the town the site for the Courthouse and Jail, the block of ground where the old cemetery used to be (now occupied in part by the Memorial Hall), also the ground on which the Mono County Hospital and Community Church now stand. He was Bridgeport's first Postmaster, a Supervisor, and he built Bryant's Hall, an old landmark now torn down. On its site stands "Slick's Motel," owned and operated by Pioneer Bryant's grandson, M. A. Bryant, and wife, and great-grandson, Daniel L. Bryant. The last named recently gave to the Catholic Church the land on which the Infant of Prague Church is built.

Until 1880 farms had increased more in size than in number. At one time in the 1890's, the Rickey Land and Cattle Company owned 12.000 acres in Bridgeport Valley alone. The other farmers used to say that Tom Rickey started his holdings with one bull and a branding iron. The Rickey Company was later dissolved into other ranches with private ownership.

Bridgeport Lake, with stalwart old Mr. Jackson at its back, now covers the ranches once owned by Charles Stewart, P. G. Hughes, W. P. Brandon, and part of the A. F. Bryant Ranch.

Two toll roads were in operation a few miles out of early Bridgeport, the one on the East Walker River, six miles down the canyon, was known as The Dardanelles Toll road. Henry Hays collected tolls on this road and lived in a comfortable house on the north side of the bridge. The site of the old toll house can well be identified by the huge straight bluff of rocks which rise across the river behind the house and which, probably, gave it the name of "The Dardanelles."

The toll house on the Bodie road was seven miles from Bridgeport. The house has fallen into decay—but opposite the house, its original site, a dug out cellar in the hill closed by heavy wooden doors, can still be seen.

The road leading to the toll house was called the Clear Water Toll Road. It was operated by John Carpenter Murphey, a pioneer, who, when crossing the plains in a covered wagon train, met and married his wife. At this toll house, the Murphey's raised a family of three sons, Ed, Lew, and John, and a daughter, Birdie.

The youngest son, John, after graduation from the University of California was elected District Attorney and later Superior Judge

Members of the Rebekah and Odd Fellows Lodges, Bridgeport, 1894

of Mono County. He served his County in this office for many years. Later he accepted a Superior Judgeship in Alameda County and made his home in Berkeley in order to educate his own children. "Johnnie" Murphey, as he was affectionately known to the people of Mono, was a symbol of all that was just and upright in a man.

Doctor Clark Sinclair, the lovable old peg-leg, was Bridgeport's first physician and surgeon. He ministered night and day to the sick people of the community. No below zero temperature kept him from answering a sick call. His wife, lovingly known as "Auntie Sinclair," assisted him as a nurse when necessary.

His great granddaughter, Mrs. Ann Utzman, and her daughter and son, still reside in Bridgeport. They are also descendants of the Wedertz family.

The social life of early Bridgeport revolved around the different lodges—The Masonic, the Independent Order of Odd Fellows, and the Rebeccas.

The I.O.O.F. brick hall, where all lodge meetings were held, is still standing on lower Main Street.

The lodges had certain times of year when they held their grand balls and celebrations in Bryant's Hall.

The masquerades were a favorite, and shrouded in much secrecy. Many a surprise and laugh was in store when finally the participants unmasked.

The square dances were lively and full of fun, punctuated by the waltzes, the schottisches, and the polkas. It was considered quite

Pacific Coast Pioneers of Bridgeport, Admission Day, 1884

1. __________ 2. H. Leavitt 3. Henry Hays 4. __________ 5. Robert Folger 6. __________ 7. J. Sawyer 8. __________ 9. Charles Stewart 10. Alex Folger 11. Judge Briggs 12. Z. B. Tinkham 13. Hayett 14. __________ 15. A. F. Bryant 16. __________ 17. O. Jones 18. Pike Richardson 19. Sam Fales 20. David Hays

an accomplishment in those days to be a good ballroom dancer.

The orchestra was made up of C. D. Heath at the piano, Clay Hampton with his violin, and Charlie Hayes sending out the high notes on his clarinet.

The Christmas Season was joyous with pre-holiday parties where popcorn was strung for the community Christmas tree.

The Fourth of July celebration is now carried on in about the same traditional way that it was observed in early Bridgeport. There were literary exercises in the morning, a barbecue at noon, street races and contests in the afternoon, and a grand ball in the evening at Bryant's Hall.

The orator of the literary exercises was generally the leading attorney of Bridgeport, W. O. Parker. He was the father of the late Patrick R. Parker who was Judge of Mono County for over twenty years. Judge Parker was widely and favorably known throughout the State as a fine jurist. Following in the footsteps of his father, he was the orator of the day at many of the later Fourth of July celebrations.

In the summer haying season, most of the ranchers and their wives solved the labor problem by making haying a co-operative project. The farmers would cut, stack, or bale the hay in the fields while their wives would help with the cooking at the ranch where the haying was in progress. "Many hands make light work" and, in this case, light hearts, too.

The quilting parties in the afternoons were a form of relaxation and sociability for the house wives. It, too, was a co-operative affair, generally held at the Leavitt House. A patch quilt was set up in the frame and was ready to be worked on at any time.

In winter the main recreations were sleighing and skating. The East Walker River was a sheet of solid ice for miles, and most of the young people became fine skaters. Some became expert enough to cut their initials in the ice while skating.

The things that happened on Halloween were uncanny—ghosts and goblins roamed the streets. (It was strange how large some of those goblins were.) Next morning when a rancher opened his stable door to let out his horses, several bellowing cows would come running out. Or, the housewife, who on going to feed her chickens found that overnight they had turned from Rhode Island Reds to White Plymouth Rocks. The out-houses had suddenly taken on legs and jumped onto the middle of Main Street or into a neighbor's yard.

In the Courthouse restrooms, the signs reading "Ladies" "Gents" had, under the witchery of night, changed places. Confusion and embarrassment resulted the following day.

The schoolhouse came in for its share of sorcery on Halloween. Several sheep sometimes shared the library overnight, much to the consternation of the teacher and the hilarity of the pupils when the library door was opened. Bales of hay rested atop the desks in the schoolroom, which pleased the pupils much more than the customary books.

The A. P. Allen's, an old couple who lived in the Colonial house on upper Main Street, kept the Bridgeporters greatly interested and inquisitive about the spiritualistic meetings held in their home. They gradually acquired a small but devout following, among them Z. B. Tinkum, the County Assessor. Mrs. Allen was the medium, speaking East Indian while in a trance. Her disciples were guided implicitly by her revelations.

So the people of early Bridgeport lived happy, but rather uneventful

Twin Lakes

ful, lives as did hundreds of thousands of other people in the early farming communities of the United States.

TWIN LAKES

To write about Bridgeport without mentioning the Twin Lakes region would be like writing about Switzerland without mentioning the Alps.

This beautiful mountain canyon has many attractions besides those of hunting and fishing, boating, water skiing and hiking.

To those who love the beauties of nature, the Twin Lakes region, with the crags and Saw Tooth Ridge as a background, is and always has been awe inspiring.

A face formed by the towering crags, looking up at the sky, is plainly visible. An Indian legend about its origin runs thus:

In ages past, the Piutes had to fight fierce battles with other tribes who lived across the mountains, and many Indians were killed. Then a big earthquake came that lasted two days and nights. The Indians were very much afraid. The Great Spirit was throwing mountains of granite rocks high up between the tribes so that they could fight no more. When the earthquake was over, one rock had a face looking at the sky. The white men now call it "The Old Man of The Mountains," but the Indians say "It is a Good Spirit

The homestead cabin of William and Dora Cargill at Upper Twin Lakes (now Mono Village)

which came to watch over the Piute tribe and keep our enemies away."

At the foot of Saw Tooth Ridge at the end of upper Twin Lake is a beautiful spot called Mono Village, fast becoming known as one of the principal resorts of Mono County. It is owned by Mr. and Mrs. Norman Annett, the latter being Alpha Day, granddaughter of Byron Day. The land was homesteaded by William Cargill and his wife Dora, daughter of Louis Wedertz. At this resort there is a large granite boulder known as "Arrow Head Rock" used by the Indians to shape their arrows. At the base of this rock, small fragments of black obsidian can still be dug up.

Between the lakes in days gone by, a dapper little man with a goatee, named Jack Westwood, made a living by selling trout at *ten cents* a pound. He lived across the river in a little wooden shack which had to be reached by a foot bridge. Jack fished early and late to supply the demand. He kept the fish alive by floating them in gunny sacks in the river. Once the County officers played a mean trick on him by having the County Sheriff engage him in conversation while several of them cut the rope that held the sacks in the river and made off with all of Jack's stock in trade.

The County officers in the early 1890's had a fine rowboat on the upper lake. As a co-operative affair, they established comfortable camping accommodations for their families on the ground between the lakes. How amazed these same people would be today if they could see the many beautiful homes which now surround these lakes.

At the end of the Lower Lake is the well-known Crag's Resort of Mr. and Mrs. Charles Honn.

This resort was developed on land taken up in the early days by Andrew Smith, for many years a millwright in the Standard Mill in Bodie. Numerous modern cabins of The Crag's Resort now surround his little home.

Buckeye Canyon, with its hot spring, was another favorite place where the early Bridgeporters could spend a pleasant day. It was a six-mile ride through green meadows and was reached by fording Robinson Creek.

An old fellow named Jim Henry had constructed three large square wooden tubs for those who wanted a bath. He had housed them in with rough boards, not minding knot holes and chinks between, and piped cold water and hot water into the tubs. He charged 35c for a bath, with wholesale rates for children.

The housewives arrived at Buckeye supplied with soap, towel, scrubbing brushes, brooms, etc., and the children were wild with excitement. No conserving of hot water here and no restriction on splashing it on the rough wooden floor. If one "kid" was found peeking in a knot hole at another, he usually got a splash of water in his eye or better still, a lump of soap that really stung.

Other scenic and beautiful canyons around Bridgeport, once inaccessible, are the Green Creek and Virginia Lake Canyons.

One of the first permanent summer homes built in this region was the home of Mr. and Mrs. J. J. Reeves at Virginia Lakes.

A mile out of Bridgeport to the southeast, there is a very interesting deposit of Travertine marble, one of the few to be found in the United States. In some places, it is still in the stages of formation

Travertine Deposits

where a hot spring comes bubbling out of the ground. Much of the marble from this deposit has been used for decoration on large buildings in San Francisco. The deposit is privately owned.

In the horse and buggy days the trip from Bridgeport to Virginia City took four days.

Starting from Bridgeport on a summer's morning, travelers spent the first night at Barnett's Hotel in Antelope Valley (Coleville). This was an interesting stop since behind the hotel was an orchard of apples, peaches, and plums; the guests being allowed to eat all they wanted. Still further back was an apiary with rows and rows of bee hives; the bees being mighty busy in alfalfa and the yellow sage seasons.

The second night was spent at the Mountain House above the "Y" to the north. The old white house, a landmark, is still standing. This was a very busy spot in the late 1880's as it was the stopping place for all the teams going to Bodie via Wellington, Nevada. It was owned by a family named Holbrook and was called Holbrook's Station.

The third night was spent at the Mormon Settlement of Genoa, generally in some private home.

The fourth day found the travelers arriving at their destination, Virginia City, via Carson City, Nevada.

The trip can now be made in less than an hour by plane and less than two hours by automobile.

Bridgeport on Highway 395 is no longer an isolated outpost.

REMINISCENCES OF EARLY BRIDGEPORT

Smell of new mown hay.

Sound of wood saws buzzing in the fall.

Hops growing in profusion around every home.

"Ammy" Bryant's old crooked-horned ram chasing the children.

Daughters of Lish Gurney, the butcher, stamping down with bare feet, sauerkraut in big wooden tubs.

Children playing hide-and-go-seek between the hay cocks.

Bushes laden with currants at the Hunewill and Elliott ranches.

Quail and snipe in the meadows.

Huge wood piles in the fall.

Near panic at the Huntoon ranch when "Mustang Maggie" (Indian) boiled all the winter woolen underwear.

Smell and glow of sagebrush fires from the Indian camps.

Clarence and Frank Wedertz cutting their initials in the ice while skating.

The cemetery in the middle of town where the Memorial Hall now stands.

Steamed windows and smell of boiling clothes.

Two little girls came often to the cemetery in town bringing wild flowers to a child's grave. On this grave a beautiful little headstone on which the name Maurice was inscribed. The little girls trying so hard to cry over the death of little Maurice who had died before they were born. One of them was his sister.

Big 20-Mule teams hauling freight to Bodie and Lundy.

Piutes selling Mono Lake ducks from house to house at 20c each.

The Sheriff auctioning off Ah Tai's stock of merchandise after his tragic death.

Piute women peeking through the windows.

Small bags of asafetida worn around the neck to ward off sickness.

Every Mahala (Indian woman) concealing in her bosom a piece of fat bacon wrapped in calico. This she pulled out several times a day, rubbing it on her face to make it glow and shine. (An aboriginal beauty treatment)—most effective.

Bodie and Lundy keeping the jail full.

Jelly making at the Elliott ranch with Fat Indian Annie throwing out the juice and saving the skins and seeds.

Little short, bewhiskered Bobby Folger trying to dance the schottish.

Toll roads—buggies—surries and lumber teams.

The Spring medicine—Sulphur and molasses.

Traveling gypsies telling fortunes. (Carrying off anything they could steal.)

Dick Bernard—ladies' man—with high hat, gloves and cane.

Cord Norst and his Indian wife from Dogtown, weighing and selling gold dust at the Dave Hays' store.

Old bachelor Sharkey eating by hand out of the frying pan when he had a guest; his only objects of utility being one knife, one fork, one spoon, one cup, one plate.

P. G. Hughes' smoldering coal pit next to his blacksmith shop. He and his son Bill always busy shoeing horses.

The burning of coyote heads in the Courthouse yard after the five dollar bounty was given the hunter.

Pike Richardson of the Brick Saloon on main street giving dimes daily to the children. "Auntie" Richardson at home taking in sewing to "make ends meet."

Excitement and joy when the heavily laden fruit teams arrived from Tuolumne County. Drivers, Marshall, Ratto and Antoninni. The latter two were lame.

"Grandma" Murphey of the toll road demonstrating on her up and down wooden churn "By the day"—slow motion. "By the contract"—fast high speed.

Swallows being shot by the County officials to keep them from building nests in the fret work of the Courthouse.

The exchanging of starters of yeast among the housewives to keep it pepped up.

School teachers who really taught the 3 R's and good Spencerian penmanship.

Snowmen that lasted all winter.

In winter, firkins (small kegs) of frozen butter with brine on top and a hammer and chisel to carve out a piece.

The trails through the snow to the outhouses in winter.

"By" Day always having gentle horses for the children to ride—gratis.

Dismal howling of coyotes on winter nights.

Encounters with skunks after which the victim had to burn his clothes.

Tall Alec and short Bobby Folger, Editors of the Weekly *Chronicle Union* dubbed "The long and the short of it."

The Indians forcasting a hard winter when the pine nut crop was abundant.

A whole Fourth of July celebration called off when two unknown sheepmen lost their lives in a cloudburst at Mormon Ranch.

The Hatfield barber shop with personal initialed shaving mugs row on row.

Formal dinners and soirees at the A. F. Bryant home.

Sam Hopkins, the carpenter, who made wooden coffins in his spare time and took refuge in one of them when "sleeping off" a drunk.

Butterick paper patterns of children's clothes, exchanged until they were worn out.

Some of the male population sneaking up to Bodie to have their fling.

Help by the whole community when anyone was in need or trouble.

Early settlers planting trout in the rivers and lakes and carp in the irrigation ditches to rid the latter of waving grass and algae.

A river flowing through green meadows where the Bridgeport Lake now stands.

Buggy whips, side saddles, and riding habits—coal oil lamps, feather beds, sleigh bells, bustles and hoops, wash boards, and home made soap.

Spring house cleaning with the "hosing" outside of the bed springs and the beating of carpets on the clothes lines.

Little "Grandma" Hunewill pulling her beautiful pansies apart, leaf by leaf, to finally show "Jack-In-His-Pulpit" to the children.

A potato stuck on the spout of a coal oil can.

These are some of the *little* things that made Bridgeport the Bridgeport of yesterday.

GEORGE HODGES -VS- McGUFFIN

George Hodges was a ranch hand of two personalities and two names, each name fitting that different personality.

When sober, he was George Hodges, the steady industrious, reliable, frugal farm hand on the Hunewill Ranch. His frugality almost reached the point of making George a miser. He washed his own clothes, patched his overalls and underwear, rolled his cigarettes, hoarded his money, and in fact never allowed George one luxury and, sometimes, even denied him the necessities of life.

His other name and personality was known as McGuffin—the drunk—the wit—the spendthrift of Bridgeport Valley.

When by dint of saving and self-denial, over a term of about two years, George Hodges had accumulated a few hundred dollars, the domineering, craving personality of McGuffin began to assert itself and HE took the upper hand.

Then George would slyly enter an old cellar, start digging in the earth and uncover a can that contained his savings.

He would come out of the cellar like a thief, knowing that McGuffin had it in his mind to dissipate the horde of hard-earned, hard-saved dollars.

George carefully counted the funds (although he knew almost to a penny what was there). "Yes, there was plenty to satisfy the demands of McGuffin."

Then George Hodges carefully dressed himself in his *one* good brown suit, saddled his horse Jerry and set out for Bridgeport. On the way down he knew that McGuffin intended "to paint the town red."

Bridgeport was a quiet little village and even the children enjoyed the excitement and merriment that McGuffin caused by his escapades. Drink sharpened, his mind, and his witticisms were beyond the telling.

He of course was welcomed at the numerous saloons and when he threw a twenty dollar gold piece on the bar the whole "house" was invited up to drink, not once but often. No one went thirsty when McGuffin was in town.

When McGuffin was "thoroughly organized," he proceeded to make the rounds of the stores. When a conscientious store keeper protested against the sale of unnecessary merchandise to McGuffin, he insisted on buying it anyway. Once it was a pair of high gum boots, and a black umbrella. Pulling on the boots, which were hip length, and raising the umbrella over his head, he paraded out of the store saying "I want to teach the people of Bridgeport to always be prepared for the rainy day."

At another time he bought all the silk neckties to be found in town and draped them around his neck, suggesting that Bridgeport should stage a "necktie party" (a hanging) as well as Bodie, and that McGuffin should be the first one to be strung up.

One day he noticed that the ground around the hitching posts where the horses were tied needed cleaning. He promptly went down to the store and bought a dozen brooms. He stood a new broom up against each hitching post in town. "Just a reminder," said McGuffin, "that out at the Hunewill Ranch I keep places like that clean."

On one occasion, his fancy ran to buggy whips. Buying all the stock in town he made a tour around to the homes. When the lady of the house answered his rap, he greeted her with a low bow, and presenting her with a buggy whip suggested that if she didn't happen to own a horse to use it on the children.

His saddle horse, Jerry, which was kept in the Waltz stable was visited daily by McGuffin and assured by a loving kiss, lumps of sugar, and petting that he hadn't been forgotten.

One day he ordered the stable boy to saddle his Jerry with a ladies' side saddle, and tying a carriage robe around his waist he proceeded to mount the horse. Jerry, being aware that his rider wasn't too steady, went very slowly up and down the street, while McGuffin kept announcing "Come and see the *modest* Godiva."

A bolt of black crepe in the Dave Hays' store didn't escape his notice and, as his spirits were rather at a low ebb that day, he bought the crepe, draping yards and yards around his hat and letting the rest of it trail behind him like a wraith. He called all the "boys" up to the bar announcing "Now all my friends are dead—so why shouldn't I go into mourning? But, we'll have a drink to them anyway, hoping they are in Heaven."

One night at a late hour, Sheriff Jim Dolan saw McGuffin, the worse for whiskey, reclining against the wall of a building. Jim, through goodness of heart, and with no intent to put McGuffin under arrest, decided to give him a warm bed in jail and sober him up, thinking he might be able to persuade him to go back to the ranch the next day. McGuffin proved to be a dead weight, but Jim was young and strong and they were making headway slowly towards the jail. Finally McGuffin rose to a sitting position as Jim stopped for breath and in a pitying tone of voice, said, "Now Jim, 'taint fair for *you* to do *all* the draggin'. You lie down and I'll drag *you* for awhile."

The next day a buck board drawn by two horses, having two passengers and a horse tied behind, was seen slowly wending its way up Hunewill Lane. The driver was Sheriff Jim Dolan, taking George Hodges and Jerry back home.

A TRIP TO FALES HOT SPRINGS IN THE 90's

Dear reader, if you would like to take a trip which is enjoyable and different and chucked full of real wholesome pleasure, let me take you from Bridgeport to Fales Hot Springs in the late eighty's or early nineties. Here you will find never-to-be-forgotten personalities, good mineral bathing, excellent food, dancing and entertainment. It sounds as if I were describing a modern resort doesn't it? Well, omit the word "modern" and that's what Fales was in its primitive, delightful way, before the turn of the century.

The Springs are located about fourteen miles north and west of Bridgeport. We go by buggy team as it is just the right distance for a day's round trip through wonderfully scenic country, giving you a thrill at each new turn in the road. You ride between placid green meadows where cattle and sheep are grazing, cross rushing streams and come close to timber covered mountains.

You catch a view of the Sierra Nevada, with their snow capped peaks some twenty miles away, framed by the rocky aperture of The Devil's Gate. Every mountainous region it seems has a Devil's Gate, but the view through this one, going towards Fales, is unsurpassed.

We suddenly come upon our first view of the Springs from the road directly above them as they are in a hollow in the hills.

The smell of minerals and steam greets us and we are conscious of warm heavy moisture in the air.

The springs bubble up from the earth in an immense pool in a turbulent, rollicking, exciting sort of a way, not throwing any gushers into the air, but emitting clouds of steam.

A Trip to Fales Hot Springs in the 90's

Further down are the baths but we have not time to think of them yet, for the folks who live here are coming out to give us a royal welcome. They are Sam, the owner, his wife, Diana, his step-daughter Minnie and brother Tom, to say nothing of the geese, turkeys, and chickens which half run, half flutter, and fly up the hill to meet us, led by patriarch of the flock, Brigham, a turkey gobbler. He rustles up his feathers, spreads out his wings until he seems double his original size, and gobbles his welcome lone and loud.

The children in our party are half delighted, half terrified by Brigham's antics.

The horses shy away from the feathered flock and the stable boy takes them off to the barn for a rest and a feed of oats, hay, and barley.

Fales is the stopping place for the big freight teams and travelers coming over the Sonora road.

You will be surprised at the number of people who are here. Some are stopping in the big two story hotel overnight, others for a longer

Fales Hot Springs

time in order to take advantage of the highly mineralized water for their various ailments.

Nearly always the first procedure of the visitors is to enjoy a bath. There is a choice of four: a tub, a steam, or mud bath, or the more active freedom of the pool bath. The tubs are wooden square affairs with water piped in from the cold and from the hot spring. Be careful, for the water is terribly hot, 180° Fahrenheit. (Only thirty feet below the hot spring the cold spring comes bubbling up.)

The mothers give the children a good scrubbing in the wooden tubs. It is so easy it seems, to them, to bathe the children here instead of at home in Bridgeport. There they have to use the old, round, wooden or galvanized tub in the middle of the kitchen floor, with water that is pumped from the well and heated on the wood stove.

The steam baths are also housed in wooden shacks. It doesn't matter if there are a few cracks in the walls, the steam makes visibility from the outside to the inside practically nil. The floor is of wooden slats placed far apart so the hot steam can come rolling up.

The slats are none too safe, as quite recently a fat elderly Irish woman from Bodie named Ellen O'Brien broke through and slightly scalded her feet. She bounded out into the open in nature's garb, throwing her arms in the air and yelling, "Shure I'll run out if awl of Bodie is lookin' afore I'll be scalded to death in the devil's mush pot."

The plunge, about 20 x 30 feet is also loosely housed. The merriment enjoyed by the bathers can be heard for some distance outside. Here all ages seem to gather for the rollicking fun of ducking and dousing.

The mud baths are seldom used.

After the baths, attention is turned to the dining room in the big building.

Diana Fales is an excellent cook. A few years ago she was a beautiful woman, but her beauty is fast fading by the hard work she is doing here.

She was a widow by the name of Clark and had supported herself and daughter Minnie by running a lodging house, first in Aurora and then in Bodie.

In the latter place she met tall and lanky Sam Fales, (many years her senior, and quite bald), and married him.

Minnie is now in her late 'teens, tall and willowy, with two long braids of blonde hair hanging down her back. She helps her mother with the cooking and various other duties around the Springs, is passionately fond of music, and plays the piano exceptionally well.

As we go into the dining room with appetites that can do justice to any meal, we see the table laden with all kinds of good home-cooked food, the piece-de-resistance of the meal is usually chicken. There are delicious fruits which are brought by heavily laden fruit wagons from Sonora. During the course of the meal, Clay Hampton, the School Master from Bridgeport, appears at the door. He is an affable, professional, looking person, noted for his fine Spencerian penmanship, drawing, and love of music. He is greeted by applause as he is carrying the case containing his "fiddle" which means there will be dancing later on. He is "sweet on Miss Minnie" who is one of his upper grade pupils.

After the sumptuous meal which costs only 50c for adults and 25c

Diana Fales

for children, (including the bath), the dining room is cleared for dancing.

Clay takes his violin out of the case and begins to tune it. Minnie shyly slips into her place at the piano. (It is no surprise to any one when, shortly afterwards, they are married.) The music starts, the fun begins, waltzes, polkas, schottishes, and square dances. How these "old-timers" hoe it down in the square dances until they are breathless. Then Tom and Sam, the two comedians, start *their* entertainment.

Sam Fales

Tom is a rather good ventriloquist and the little papier mache dummy on his lap knows all the answers. The children are spell-bound and crowd around. "Don't get too close," he tells them, "as Chester doesn't like it." The real thrill comes when Santa Claus calls down through the chimney to know their names and what they want for Christmas. They all answer at once, but Santa doesn't seem to mind that.

Then Sam pulls up his barroom chair on the right hand side of the fire place where the legs fit exactly into the grooves they have made in the floor. It is from this vantage point he practices the "art" of tobacco spitting for many hours each day at the targets drawn on the sides of the fire place. So perfect has he become that he is now the acknowledged champion tobacco spitter in these parts, and seldom has anyone to challenge him.

He is also noted as a spinner of tall, blood curdling, yarns of his own imagination, but he has two rivals in this field, Sam Clemens (Mark Twain) in Aurora and "Lying" Jim Townsend in Bodie.

Tonight no one comes forth to challenge him in the tobacco spitting contest. So he displays his talent anyway for the amusement of the visitors. Two men are laying wagers in the back of the room as to his hits and misses. After this he is called on for a story. He thinks it best to tell a true one first as it sort of throws folks off guard for those that follow. So he begins:

"The place where we are now sitting was a large Indian encampment ground in its day. Hundreds of Piutes made these Springs their home, as it was the warmest place to be found hereabouts, and fish and game were plentiful.

"On the hill directly in front of this building the grinding bowls the Indians used are still to be seen hewn in the solid granite—and there they will be 'till the end of time. After a rain the birds come and drink out of them as the Red men will never be here to use them anymore."

Sam, at this point, seems to realize he is getting into a sentimental mood which he rather despises, so he aims the ammunition he has been gathering at the furtherest target—and hits it.

A pause.

"Now folks I want to tell you of a serious injury that happened to me once. One below zero morning I looked out and saw the hot springs *all frozen over.* I was so surprised I rushed out in my stocking feet. The ice was thick. Thinking it would hold me up, I started to cross. In the middle of the pool, the ice cracked and broke. My feet were so badly scalded I wasn't able to walk for months. During the time of my disability I decided to try my hands at inventing. I worked for months on an invention of perpetual motion. Sort of a pendulum affair. First it seemed to go and then it wouldn't. But, believe it or not, I finally discovered it"—a pause—"It was a woman's tongue."

Another round of tobacco juice hit its mark. Then he continues, "At one time we knew the Indians were on the warpath all around the country. We were laying low, hoping they would move to other parts as winter was coming on.

"The time came when we had to go into the timber land to get wood. Looking down the mountain we saw them coming hooping and hollering like a pack of devils. We knew we must ride for our lives as we were outnumbered twenty to one. We finally ended up in a box canyon with our back to a cliff, and they killed *every one of us*—to the *last man*."

A sweet old lady screams and nearly faints at Sam's dramatic ending of this story.

It is now time for us to say good night and depart for Bridgeport. The ride home is like going through fairyland as there is a full moon.

Gone now are all the actors in the drama of that day long past. Gone is the old hotel, a landmark of Pioneer days, as it burned down quite recently.

Today the Springs only are unchanged, and around them is being built a more modern resort having great potentialities.

THE FOLGERS

Robert M. and Alexander C. Folger, early editors of the official paper of Mono County—The Bridgeport *Chronicle-Union*, were the most fastidious gentlemen of the community. Their speech was soft, their manners impeccable.

Bobby and Alex, as they were affectionately called, were always immaculate in high, starched collars, frock coats, and striped trousers. (Ah, shades of Robert and Alex in your frock coats! Are you gazing down on your Bridgeport these summer days where the streets are full of men running around in calico shorts?)

Alex was tall and thin and did most of the editing of the paper. He was married to a gentle little lady who was never seen without a white kerchief placed flat around her neck. This, coupled with the attire, speech, and manners of the Folgers led to the supposition by the townsfolk that they were Quakers.

Bobby was short, rather stout in figure, and did most of the strenuous work in the office, as this was the day of hand presses and the papers had to be folded over and over.

Then there was the brown horse, a gentle animal called Jinny, which was so beloved by the Folgers that they considered her to be almost a member of the family. She was always spoken of in the most loving terms, all her virtues extolled. No conversation was complete or interesting to the Folgers without mention of Jinny.

Bobby rose early each morning and went to Jinny's stall. She was given two lumps of sugar, then hay and oats, and while she was enjoying this repast, Bobby would brush and curry her shiny coat.

On summer evenings, Bobby would hitch Jinny to the family buggy, the top of which was adorned with deep black fringe, and being the driver, would take his place in the front seat, and Alex and his wife would sit in back.

So the three Folgers, and their buggy drawn by Jinny, were a familiar sight around early Bridgeport for many years, Jinny never going at any pace faster than a walk.

The first printing office was on Main Street, but after a time, the brothers decided on a new building. This was built on School Street, a little to the north and west of the Courthouse.

The printing office in front was large, due to the cumbersome presses of that period. Comfortable living quarters were built back of the office. No expense was spared to build a nice, warm, padded stable for Jinny, out in the yard.

Alex and Bobby, being patriotic souls, wanted a flag flying over their place of business. They hired Indians to scout around the mountains and bring in the tallest, straightest pine tree they could find. This was dressed down for a flag pole, the highest one in Mono County.

The flag raising of the Folgers was a most eventful one. It was scheduled just before July 4th. Local talent furnished the music. The Star Spangled Banner and America were played as the flag was hoisted aloft. Alex gave a short speech. There was community singing of well known songs. The children in their Fourth of July finery joined hands and circled around the flag pole. Refreshments were served by little white-kerchiefed "Grandma Folger." The flag raising over the Chronicle-Union building was a memorable event in Bridgeport.

Life for the Folgers went smoothly for some years. Then tragedy struck. Bobby, on going out to the stable one morning, found Jinny dead. She was swollen to twice her size. It was decided by the farmers, who understood such cases, that her death was caused by cholic from eating alfalfa that had been frozen. There was real grief in the Folger household.

Some Indians were hired to dig a grave for Jinny in the back yard. The mound above her was piled high—too high—but Bobby and Alex did not take notice of this. They had a wooden board place at the head of the grave inscribed:

"Our Beloved Jinny—The Faithful"

The barn was closed, never to be opened again. The carriage was covered over and put away.

One morning in the following spring, Bobby discovered something that shocked him and made him sick at heart. Jinny's grave had been desecrated. The coyotes had found it and dug down. Four white stumps were sticking up like sentinals—nothing but bone and hoof. The Indians had dug a much too shallow grave. Sorrowfully, Bobby broke the news to Alex and Grandma Folger—What was to be done? The only solution was to saw off the legs and place them in the grave beside Jinny. Those legs that had cheerfully and faithfully carried the Folgers on the evening rides—the only one pleasure which they had really ever known.

Some years later, the Folgers moved away and the *Chronicle-Union* changed hands, as it has done many times since; however, it is still published under its original name.

THE PIUTE INDIANS REVENGE ON AH QUONG TAI

On June 9, 1891, the most tragic and terrifying event occurred in Bridgeport that has ever been known, or probably ever *will* be known in this peaceful little valley.

People talk of it to this day, and refer to it as the "Beheading of Ah Quong Tai."

I, the author of this book, was an eye witness to happenings in this tragedy, and although only nine years of age to the day, the memory of the gruesome climax and the events leading up to it, are indelibly impressed upon my mind.

The reason I knew many of the inside facts was that my father, M. J. Cody, was Sheriff of Mono County at the time, and the details of what was taking place were reported and discussed in our home.

I know seven persons, still living, who were in Bridgeport during those days of anxiety and sleepless nights, and I will quote throughout the story from a signed statement by the late D. W. Hays of Alberta, Canada, a noted Hydraulic Engineer for the English Government, who was born in Bridgeport and who spent his boyhood here. Another person with whom I have often discussed this Indian uprising is Lottie Towle Bernard, who, as a child, ran with me to the front of the Courthouse in order to see the wild, howling, savage mob dragging their victim up Main Street. The events that led up to this scene I will endeavor to describe in sequence to you, the reader.

On June 2, 1891, a delegation of Walker River Piute Indians from the Reservation in Nevada, headed by Captain Charlie, came into Bridgeport to get Captain Jim and the Bridgeport Indians to help them locate a missing member of their tribe, known as Poker Tom.

Tom had not been seen or heard of since about the middle of April when it was known he had gone to Bridgeport and had played poker with a Chinese merchant by the name of Ah Quong Tai. At A. F. Bryant's store he had bought a piece of calico, telling some Indians, whom he met, that he had won $50.00 from Ah Tai the night before and was going home before he got into another game and lost it.

Subsequent events proved that Tom had weakened, and had again sought out Ah Tai, who probably had more tricks up his sleeve than did Bret Harte's "Heathen Chinee."

Ah Tai owned a store across the river from the main part of town. He was a small Chinese with a long queue that he sometimes wore coiled up on his head and sometimes let hang where it would almost reach the floor. This delighted the children who called it Ah Tai's "pigtail."

As soon as the reason for the Nevada Walker Reservation Piutes being in Bridgeport became noised around town, the Bridgeport Indians began to congregate in groups ready to assist their Reservation brothers in locating Tom.

Captain Charlie of the Nevada Indians asked all the Piutes to come across the bridge to Indian town where he could hold a pow

Ah Quong Tai, killed by Indians June 9, 1891 at Bridgeport

wow. The excited throng lost no time in doing this. The Indians squatted down on their haunches, some of them almost hidden by sage brush. One by one as they were called, they arose and gave their testimony which really amounted to nothing. At the end of each recital, they would all set up a loud gabble, gabble, in their own language, gesticulating wildly with their hands in anticipation of finding the body of Poker Tom. It was finally agreed that a search for Tom should be made, in the fields and on the hills, by all the Indians. The sage brush court adjourned and the Piutes ran in all directions, some of them even getting out their saddle horses. They were keyed up to such a pitch of excitement it was like a contest, to see who would come upon the remains of Poker Tom first. Spreading out over the Valley in all directions, it was not long before one of them discovered Tom's saddle blanket and bundle of calico in Bryant's field, north of town, where it was known he had staked his horse at the time he was last seen here.

Sheriff Cody, who had been assisting the Indians in the search, took these pieces of evidence to his office.

The findings of these effects added fuel to the excitement already raging and the Indians held another frenzied meeting, where they openly accused Ah Quong Tai of the murder and vowed to avenge Tom's death.

Sheriff Cody, who had gained their confidence, and whom they called "The White Chief," reasoned with them after this meeting and they finally promised to camp beyond the bridge and create no disturbance that night.

By this time, not only the Nevada Indians but all the Piutes of the region, several hundred strong, had assembled in Bridgeport. The frightened "Whites," who were greatly outnumbered, had a hard time feeding them as they came to every house demanding "hog-a-di"—which they ate sitting on the wood piles.

The two hotels, who charged them twenty-five cents for a meal, served behind the building, were busy night and day.

On June 4th, another pow-wow was held and the Indians decided to patrol the river and drag it in the deep places. They used long flimsy poles for this. Nothing was found until they reached Bryant's dam, clinging to which they found a black water-logged coat belonging to Tom. On finding this, this searching party gave a yell, making all believe, who heard it, that the body of Tom had been found.

The Mahalas (Indian Women) who were in camp began their

loud cries and dismal lamentations for the dead, after which they let their curiosity get the better of them and they suddenly stampeded and made a rush for the dam.

Bryant's wire fence stood in their way and greatly impeded their progress, and the squaws, in bright calico dresses, were caught and held by the barbed wire fence, some standing, others kneeling, in water up to their knees. Let it be told to the discredit of the County officers, some of whom were looking on, that not one of them was gallant enough to go to the rescue of these dusky maidens, but instead were greatly amused to the point of loud laughter at the scene.

This was the *one* small piece of comedy that was injected into an otherwise doleful tragedy.

At this time, the authorities made an investigation of Tai's store and premises. A small back room was given much attention. It was generally used for playing cards and was furnished with a table and chairs, a small bed, and a stove.

On the wall were a number of guns that the Indians had "soaked" to Ah Tai for "grub."

Pasted over the wallpaper in several places the Sheriff noticed clean new sheets of wrapping paper. On removing this wrapping paper, spots and discolorations were found underneath on the wall paper. On the floor were two boards which also showed stains, and had evidently been scrubbed. These boards and pieces of paper were later taken to the Sheriff's office as evidence.

At this stage, Ah Quong Tai was closely questioned, and although he admitted having played cards with Poker Tom on the night he disappeared, he disclaimed any knowledge of his present where-abouts. However, by this time the Indians were on the war-path for Tai, and he realized he was a doomed man.

On June 6th, after a four-day search and dragging of the river, the torso of a human being was found in the river, near the Toll House on the Sweetwater Road. I hereby quote from the typewritten signed letter of D. W. Hays of Alberta, Canada:

"My Uncle, Maurice Hayes, had occasion to deliver a small load of hay a few miles below town and took my cousin Maurice and me with him. Near our destination, we were stopped by three or four excited Indians who said they had found a part of a man in the river. My Uncle took off his shoes and socks, rolled up his pants, and waded out. There against a rock to which it had been washed, was the trunk of a human. The head had been removed, both arms cut off near the shoulders, the body had been severed below the waist, and the chest cavity was empty.

"My Uncle tied a rope to the trunk and anchored it to the shore, wrote a note to the Sheriff and officials in town and told the Indians to deliver it as soon as possible. We proceeded to our destination and delivered the hay. On our way back to town we found the Indians gone and the trunk removed. Upon arriving in town we saw a number of white men and Indians assembled in an empty building across from my father's store. An investigation was under way.

"It was found by medical examination that the trunk had been pickled, that is to say, salted down as for corned beef."

When this word reached the Indians, many of them recalled that some time previous, when eating at Ah Tai's, as was their custom, a strange kind of pickled meat with a sweet taste had been fed to them. They asked Ah Tai at the time what kind of meat it was and were told that it was "goat."

The cellar of Ah Tai's house was investigated. Many large barrels that smelled of brine were there, but they were empty.

Now being convinced that Ah Tai had fed them the flesh of Poker Tom, the Indians' anger reached a war-path pitch. They *demanded* that Ah Tai be turned over to them as, some time previous to this, the Piutes had surrendered to the Whites for trial an *Indian* Jake Gilbert who had murdered a *white* rancher, Louis Sammann, at Mono Lake. They also had turned over to the *white* authorities the *Indian* who had murdered an Antelope Valley (Coleville) Chinese.

It would be but fair to them, the Piutes said, for the whites to turn over to them a Chinese who had evidently killed one of *their* tribe, and let them deal with him accordingly. If the "whites" would not do this, said Captain Charlie, they would suffer an Indian massacre and their town would be burned.

An inquest was held on Sunday afternoon in the Superior Court room, according to the records, a jury having previously examined Ah Tai's store and buildings.

Then Ah Tai was put on the stand at this inquest. He admitted having played cards with Poker Tom, but emphatically denied that he had killed him. When shown the human torso he expressed the opinion that it was "mutton."

Frank Hanson testified at the inquest that Ah Tai had wanted to hire him to defend him if necessary, and to him, Tai admitted killing Tom with a club after they had had a quarrel in which Ah Tai had won back Poker Tom's money of the night before.

P. M. Hayes also testified that Tai had confessed his guilt to him. However, Tai stuck to his story and pleaded *"not guilty,"* but he became so panicky that he sought the protection of the jail.

The officials, aware of potential trouble, put him in jail and asked for volunteers to guard the jail, until time when Tai could be brought to trial.

Great numbers of Indians started in the evening to congregate around the jail and the sheriff's residence which adjoins the jail. After a few hours they stretched out on the ground touching hand to hand to form a human chain in order that Ah Tai could not be taken away under cover of darkness.

Being the oldest of four small children, the writer can still experience the feelings of fear and horror of that night.

The following evening, *my father*, Sheriff Cody, moved our family downtown to the Leavitt Hotel (now the Bridgeport Hotel) for the night. The children were put to bed and the "grown-ups" kept vigil.

My Father made many trips to Indian town during the night to talk with Captain Charlie of Nevada, and Captain Jim of the Bridgeport Indians, and to ask them to quell an uprising.

The next morning when we came home from the hotel, Liza Charlie, a mahala who worked for us, whispered to my mother "You no tell this. No tell Cody. Last night Indians setum heap fires all around houses in Bridgeport. Maybe this many. (She held her hands up, fingers outstretched and closed her fingers five or six times, indicating fifty or sixty.) If white man *no* give Chinaman to Indians, mahalas light fires *quick*, burn down all houses, Piute men kill all

Bridgeport Jail

white people." "You wouldn't burn down our house, would you, Liza?" asked my mother. "You and your husband, Pretty Charlie, are our friends. You have worked here for a long time." "No, I no burn down *your* house" she answered with a benign smile. "I burn down 'nother woman's house."

The Indians kept repeating that they had no grievance with the whites, providing Ah Tai was turned over to them.

On Monday, Tai engaged Judge J. C. Murphey and W. O. Parker to defend him. On Tuesday morning his preliminary examination commenced in the Justice Court, before Justice of the Peace Thomas Fales. The prisoner was in the charge of Constable Crowell.

Deputy District Attorney Hayes appeared for the people.

When the prisoner was taken into the Justice Court room in the brick building, (now occupied by a sporting goods store), hundreds of Indians posted themselves on Main Street and surrounded the building.

An account published by the *Chronicle-Union* the following week, June 13, 1891 states: "There were also many Indians mounted on horses to give pursuit, in case a move was made to take Tai out of town." It states further: "Dr. T. A. Kables, County Physician, was put on the stand and testified that while the body was that of an adult, it was cut below the thoracic cavity so that no one could tell whether it was a man or a woman. Second, also that no one could tell whether it was the remains of an Indian or not.

Some Indians were called to testify but their testimony showed nothing, so with this evidence, the prosecution closed.

Counsel for the defendant moved that the Court discharge the prisoner on the following grounds:

First—there had been no evidence to show that an Indian by the name of Poker Tom had been murdered.

Second—the evidence for the prosecution shows that they do not know whether the remains found are those of a man or a woman.

Third—there is no testimony taken before this Court as required by law.

The defendant was ordered discharged for want of sufficient evidence."

At first Ah Tai did not seem to comprehend what this discharge meant, but when informed by W. O. Parker, his counsel, that he was free and could go, Ah Tai grabbed onto Parker's arm with such force that the marks he made remained for several days.

He began to yell that he would pay $5.00 a day to any man who would guard him.

The Indians who had been in the Court room ran to both front and back doors and flung them wide open. They yelled to the horde outside in their own language, and that horde swarmed in and grabbed Ah Tai.

Justice Fales and W. O. Parker begged them not to commit a crime in the Court room.

Ah Tai was still attempting to cling to Parker with a death grip, but the Indians dislodged him, and with shouts of fiendish glee and revenge they dragged him outside and up the street. Their plans had been made in advance.

This day being the writer's birthday, my Mother had invited a number of little girls to a party, thinking the diversion would help get their minds off the gruesome things that were happening. Hearing the shouting and commotion in the street, we ran to the front of the Courthouse yard and saw Ah Tai being dragged up the street by the wild, howling mob.

I here again quote from D. W. Hays' account of the final scene:

"Adjoining my Father's premises to the west and fronting Main Street, was a livery stable and large corral. Branding of colts was in progress, to which I was a spectator sitting on the fence next to the street. Suddenly, violent screams were heard, attracting everyone's attention.

"We witnessed the Indians bringing Ah Tai from the brick building in the middle of Main Street. He appeared to be held by a man on each arm and partly dragged. His screams were being stifled by sand being thrown into his mouth. It is to be hoped that he fainted.

"The Indians proceeded up the street a further distance, then turned North at the Thomas Kirkwood home to a point about a thousand feet to "By" Day's field. White people had followed to about as far as the Courthouse.

From my vantage point of the second floor I saw the final act.

Ah Tai was dismembered, in apparently the same way Poker Tom had been. The various parts of his body were thrown aloft and scattered into the surrounding sage brush. His head was severed from his body. An Indian took hold of the queue and swinging the head in a circle let it fly."

The Reservation Indians left town immediately—the local Indians did not show up for days.

Dr. Kables, County Physician, had the parts of Ah Quong Tai gathered up and put in a blanket. They were buried in the Sinnamon Field across the road from the scene of the crime.

Several months after the death of Ah Quong Tai, the dogs belonging to "By" Day dragged home a long black braided queue attached to a small shriveled scalp lock. This they had evidently dug up in the Sinnamon Field. "By" Day flung it over a rafter in his barn where it attracted much attention for awhile.

Some time later W. H. Metson, a prominent lawyer from San Francisco, visited the "By" Day's. His sister, Mrs. Josie Lindberg, was helping organize a small museum in a room on the ground floor of the Fairmont Hotel. At Attorney Metson's request, he was given this relic to be placed in this museum.

On a recent inquiry by the writer, the museum had been moved and Ah Tai's scalp lock and queue could not be found. Wherever it is today, may it rest in peace.

CHAPTER SEVEN

Lundy

In 1878, W. J. Lundy started operating a sawmill on the lake that bore his name. He was kept busy supplying lumber for the then booming camp of Bodie, about twenty miles to the north-east.

As was the usual thing in those days prospectors were combing the mountains for gold. Three men named Wasson, Nye, and Horner came upon some good croppings of ore. They sent over to Bodie for a mining expert named G. J. McClinton and, with his help, the Homer Mining District of Mono County was organized, but the little settlement was called Lundy.

The town was so quaint, situated on the upper end of a lake, surrounded by the majestic beauties of nature, that one wondered if God had put gold too "in them thar hills."

Numerous claims were staked out, but the one that really proved to be a mine was the May Lundy, with a production of over $200,-000. It was perched like an eagle's nest on a hill so steep that a squirrel could hardly climb it.

It had a mill and boarding house, and generally the miners came to town prepared to "paint the town red."

A telegraph line was built to Bodie as early as 1880. C. F. Hector ran the pioneer stage line daily to the then booming mining camp. A large mercantile store was owned and operated by A. L. Butter-field. Mr. & Mrs. Al Taylor were proprietors of the Lake View Hotel. There were numerous other little businesses and two of the old type saloons of the mining camp days with swinging doors that never were locked.

The saloons were owned by Jack Murray and George Fry and were the respective hold outs and headquarters for the two rival gangs of toughs who kept the town somewhat in terror with their shooting frays.

Lundy

May Lundy Mine

Gang No. 1 had as its leader one Kirk Steve and, the other, Charlie Jardine, who had a record and was known through-out the West as an all around bad and dangerous character.

There had been a little, painted Chinese girl named Ling Loi in the underground of Chinatown all summer. She was leaving on a certain day for San Francisco, by stage from Lundy, supposedly taking all her earnings with her.

The Jardine gang entered into a conspiracy to kidnap her off the stage, rob her of her money, and hold her for $2,000 ransom, which they were sure the Chinese in Lundy would pay.

One of their gang, Tex Wilson, was hired to do the job.

The stage was held up by Tex, much to the consternation of the passengers, but Ling Loi obeyed orders and got off. Tex made her get up behind him on his horse, and together they went to a lonely cabin high up in the mountains where Tex previously had stored some food away.

A few nights later, Charlie Jardine showed up. Tex had a sad story to tell. Ling Loi had sent all her money to San Francisco by Wells Fargo Express except a few dollars which she needed for the trip. Jardine's news was no better. The Chinese had refused to pay the $2,000 ransom to get Ling Loi back, as another girl had already taken her place and was all the rage.

Tex and Jardine kept looking at each other in a sort of dumbfounded way with the little "Chink" girl sitting there on a log between them.

Jardine knew he was suspected and being shadowed by the Kirk Steve gang, so decided the best thing to do was to take Ling Loi to the road and let her walk back to Lundy. She and Tex went down on horse back to the same place where Tex had held up the stage. He sort of felt lonesome when Ling Loi headed on foot for Lundy and he turned his horse in the opposite direction for Mono Lake, about 6 or 7 miles distant.

Ling Loi got into Chinatown by midnight and of course told the whole story.

The Kirk Steve gang were full of whiskey in George Fry's saloon and started right out on horse back after Tex Wilson. They found

Lonely cabins on Lundy mountains

him sleeping in a dry wash near Mono Lake and got the drop on him. They brought Tex back to Lundy, his arms tied fast to his sides, and there were threats of lynching him as he was bound and tied behind the bar in George Fry's saloon.

Some of the decent men in town, lead by S. B. Burkham, fearing a lynching, sent to Bridgeport for help. Sheriff Kinney sent his Deputy Sheriff Wilcox and six other newly deputized men to cope with the situation.

They left with only Tex in hand cuffs, which infuriated the Kirk Steve gang as they thought Jardine and his followers had used Tex for their tool.

When Kirk Steve met Jardine outside the saloon the next day, the shooting started. Kirk was the worse off from liquor, and Jardine shot him in the stomach. Kirk pulled himself to his feet and with blood running into his shoes, shot Jardine in the back as he ran. Jardine fell wounded to the floor. Dr. Walker came over from Bodie and after some weeks Kirk Steve and Jardine were able to walk around, although the community would have been better off without them. They did not prefer charges against each other as they both would have landed in jail.

Jardine shortly afterward was arrested for his part in the kidnapping and taken to Bridgeport for trial.

Joe Lee, a bartender in Jack Murray's Saloon was a great admirer of Jardine. He kept antagonizing a character named Callahan by telling how Kirk Steve should have been strung up long ago and his hide and tallow given to the coyotes. Callahan was drinking in front of the bar one night and getting tired of Joe Lee's tirade. Callahan hit Lee square in the face with the butt end of his gun. Lee staggered for a minute and, reaching down for his gun under the bar, he shot Callahan square in the abdomen, and Callahan dropped to the floor mortally wounded. There was a free for all fight with guns popping every place until some far sighted miner shot the lights out.

Lee was lodged in the Bridgeport Jail next day with his pals Jardine and Tex. It wasn't a long time afterward that they sawed their way out.

Tex made his escape to Mono Lake on a horse he stole. A price was put on his head. An Indian hiding in ambush got the drop on Tex and received the reward. Judge Briggs gave Tex a long term in prison where he finally died. The two others gave themselves up.

Joe Lee, through the help of relatives, engaged Pat Reddy to defend him. He got off with a sentence of nine years in San Quentin. But the worst miscarriage of justice was that Charlie Jardine got off scott-free. He kept hanging around Bodie unemployed.

Bodie had a new Deputy Sheriff at the time. He was nicknamed Pioche Kelley as he came from Pioche, Nevada. He was known as a sure shot and rather a tough hombre himself.

The Bodie-Hawthorne stage was held up one night shortly afterwards and robbed of a shipment of bullion. All evidence pointed to Charlie Jardine as being the hold-up man. Pioche made his brags around town next day that he would "take" Jardine dead or alive. They met in an alley back of the Sawdust Corner Saloon. Each man pulled his gun but Kelley was quicker on the draw and Charlie Jardine dropped to the sidewalk dead. Pioche Kelley was acquitted the next day and given a vote of thanks by the jury for ridding the County of a character like Charlie Jardine. (The criminal records of Mono County will show this whole story to be true.)

After getting rid of the two law-breaking, gun-pulling gangs, Lundy became somewhat of a regular little mining camp with only an occasional saloon brawl now and then.

AVALANCHES

During a severe winter that brought deep snows, the people in Lundy were in constant fear of an avalanche.

In March, 1882, in six, not too widely separated places, these messengers of death and destruction came roaring down the mountain sides bringing untold tons of snow and ice and completely demolishing anything that stood in their paths. Four men were killed in the snow slide on March 15, 1882, at the foot of the May Lundy tramway. Others were imprisoned until almost dead. Many acts of heroism by persons in the rescue parties were recorded in the Minder Index of that time.

The women and children were sometimes housed for days in a building that was out of the path of snow slides and considered safe.

A letter recently received, written by a friend of ours, Oliver J. Kirkpatrick, residing in Palm Springs, is hereby quoted:

Palm Springs, Nov. 22nd, 1959

"My dear Victor & Ella,

I certainly will only be too glad to give you such information as I remember of the old town of Lundy. I was only 4 years old the year of the bad slides, 1882, but I suppose that a lot of information was later impressed on my mind by conversations of my elders. People in town were worried about the conditions at that time especially as I remember this was a heavy fall of light snow on top of the old crusted snow and dry at that. Our house was closer to the Lake than the other houses and was built in this location as a precaution against slides. We had a house full that night as our house was considered out of the snow slide belt.

Mr. and Mrs. Dick Pierce were among the crowd and Dick went to the front door to see how conditions were. Just as he opened the door a slide came from across the cañon and hit the bluff over the old hotel. I can remember his saying "There goes Chinatown." The explosion of the snow hitting the bluff sent it flying in the air across to our house. The force and volume was broken up and caused a vacuum which would not allow the shuting of the door or allow us to take a breath. I forgot how much snow came in the door, but I do know that we had a very scared crowd for a few moments, and there was a hustling to get brooms, etc. to get the snow outside.

If you think of anything more that I have not covered, address will be the same.

Best regards to all of you.

Also Merry Christmas.

Oliver"

Some time after the turn of the Century, a power house and several buildings were constructed some distance below Lundy Lake on a site where snow slides were known to be frequent.

On March 7, 1911, an avalanche of immense proportions came tearing down the mountain side carrying away the power house and buildings and burying everything in its path.

Seven men were killed instantly, buried under tons and tons of ice and snow.

A rescue crew had gathered and they worked frantically for over sixty hours finally extracating from a demolished building an unconscious woman, Mrs. R. H. Mason. A rafter that had held above her head was all that had stood between her and death. Her husband was dead in bed beside her. On account of a contact she had made with her foot on his dead body, she had to have her leg amputated.

The Homer Miner Index, a weekly newspaper, was published in Lundy by that great wit and humorist James (Lying Jim) Townsend who later published the Bodie Miner Index.

People waited outside of his printing office door until copies of his paper came off the press. A subscriber's feelings were not spared in his story telling, neither were his own feelings spared, but rather gratified, by telling outrageous tales on himself; his favorites being his monstrous capacity for liquor and its results. Many contemporary

Rescue party after avalanche with Mrs. Mason on sled

editors quoted Jim Townsend in their papers. Had he not lived in such an isolated region with a limited circulation of his paper, he no doubt would have become noted as one of the great humorists of his time. It is supposed he was the inspiration for Bret Harte's "Plain Language from Truthful James" and that Mark Twain during his Aurora days gleaned many a story from Jim Townsend.

Mining went on rather steadily in Lundy for the first three years from 1880 on and then intermittently. On November 4th, 1921, R. T. Pierce and Tom Hannah bought for taxes all the mining property of the Crystal Lake Gold Mining Company, which included the May Lundy Mine.

R. T. Pierce had been Superintendent of the May Lundy Mine during its productive years and still had faith in the property.

Tom Hannah was the son-in-law of John Muir, the naturalist. Hannah had become interested in Mono County from hearing John Muir tell of the yearly trecks he and his pal and friend William Keith used to make into the Sierra Nevada Mountains around Lundy. He (Muir) would lie on his stomach and write, while observing bird life, and William Keith would sit on a rock and paint a canvas of magnificent scenery. The John Muir trail traverses the higher elevations of the Sierras of Mono County dividing them into east and west.

As mining costs had risen so high, Pierce and Hannah did not make the May Lundy pay; so after giving it a fair trial, they closed it down.

Lundy which now has a resort with boats and motel accommodations is only 6 miles off Highway 395, east of Mono Lake.

The gold excitements of Lundy are no more. Gone is the little settlement, its bad men, its Chinatown, its red shirted miners, but the lure of its majestic mountain peaks, its streams, its lake, its verdure, will live on forever in the minds of all who visit it.

BENNETTVILLE

Some ten or eleven miles back of Lundy was the little settlement called Bennettville which was laid out to be the headquarters for the Tioga Mining District and which became a ghost town almost before it became alive. The operation of the mines in this belt caused no end of excitement and interest in Mono County in the early 1880's.

In 1860, the outcroppings of the "Great Silver Belt" were discovered on Tioga Hill, and a location made by "Doc" G. W. Chase. However Chase did more talking about the Silver Belt than he did work and took himself off to the more exciting *gold* rushes. Perhaps it was the lack of money, lack of energy or the immensity and flint-like hardness of the croppings, that discouraged him, or perhaps the assays he made did not come up to his expectations.

The existence of this ledge was known around the Mother Lode country of Mariposa and Calaveras Counties for some years.

In 1874 a boy named Brusky from Sonora was up in the moun-

Bennettville in 1902 with Mt. Dana in the distance. Photo by Celia Crocker Thompson

tains on Tioga Hill tending sheep for his father. He took samples from the ledge. As the assays did not show sufficient values to satisfy his father, no work was done. In 1875 young Brusky returned, sank a small hole on the ledge and got some better assays. On August 2, 1878, Brusky still thinking about the ledge, came back to Tioga Hill and located four claims of 1500 feet each along what he called "The Sheepherder Lode." These were subsequently purchased after his death by the Great Sierra Consolidated Silver Company. Brusky committed suicide on August 28, 1881.

O. H. Brooks who had been around Bodie had great faith in the Tioga Hill property and was its principal promoter. He went East and succeeded in getting "The Great Sierra Consolidated Silver Company of Illinois" organized to work the Sheepherder and Great Sierra Lode. Its capital stock was 800,000 shares at $10 per share or a capitalization of 8 million dollars.

He reported on coming back that the men who made up this

Company were as rich as Croesus, and a second Virginia City would spring up on Tioga Hill.

Among the principal stockholders were Thomas Bennett, Jr., founder of the Wamsutta Mills, Wm. Swift, whale ship owner and packer, his brother R. N. Swift, and William H. Forbes, one of the organizers of the American Bell Telephone Company. Thomas Bennett was the Company's president and for him the little settlement was named.

The Company tried to bring the first heavy machinery in over the mountains from Lundy. When a dozen men had spent *three* months with block and tackle, sledges and hammers, and all the manpower they possessed, to hoist ten tons of machinery over sheer cliffs from 7000 feet up to 12,000 feet, it was decided a road would have to be built. This road, called the Great Sierra Wagon Road, was built not through Lundy but on the western slope of the Sierra, *following in many places* or *being part of the Tioga-Yosemite road today.* It was about 57 miles in length with Crocker's Station as its terminus. It cost around $60,000. Part Chinese labor from the Mother Lode was employed.

In 1883 things were not going well for the Great Sierra Company at Tioga. A tunnel nearly 1,800 feet deep had been dug into hard, almost impenetrable, rock, mostly by hand power, but no ledge of great value had been cut. In all more than $300,000 had been expended.

On July 3, 1884 word came to suspend all operations. Reluctantly the miners went down the pass into Lundy to seek employment elsewhere.

There stands today amid the majestic mountains of this region old cabins, machinery and relics of the past to attest to this "Grave Yard of Lost Hopes" that once was Bennettville, Tioga Mining District of Mono County, California.

CHAPTER EIGHT

Masonic

Masonic lies about twelve miles northeast of Bridgeport and created quite a stir in the mining world when its ledges were discovered around the turn of the Century.

It was lying dormant when Aurora, Bodie, and Lundy were having their booms. A boy named Green found rich gold croppings on the Jump Up Joe, which was bought by Warren Loose of Bodie in 1901. On July 4, 1902, J. S. Phillips, Caleb Dorsy, and J. M. Bryan located the ledge on the Pittsburg Liberty. Two years later they started to mine, and built a cyanide plant. Fifty men were put to work.

The first settlement called Middle Town grew up in this section. It had a boarding house, a general store, a few dwellings, and a post office called Masonic. Lucky is the person who now has an envelope with the post mark "Masonic, Cal" on it as they are greatly sought after today by collectors of cancelled envelopes.

In turn, nearly all other properties were located and worked by private individuals from Bodie and Bridgeport. Two other little settlements were called Lower Town and Upper Town, although they consisted of perhaps a few claims and a group of cabins.

The mineralized zone extends for about three miles and has only been scratched.

The Chemung mine, on the extreme western end of Masonic, has been a good producer, but has been in the throes of litigation many times. Three different mills on the property have been torn down for different reasons.

At the present time, there is a mill on the property and some little work being done.

Middle Town, Masonic

It is hard to tell what the production of Masonic has been, as it was mined by so many private interests. However, great faith in this district still remains; which faith will no doubt be justified, when the gold mining industry so long discriminated against, comes into its own.

CHAPTER NINE

Mono Lake

Mark Twain's impressions of Mono Lake, as written in "Roughing It," were formed at a time when he and Cal Higby were worn out, tired, and disappointed in their futile search to find The Lost Cement Mine of Mono County.

Had Sam Clemmens (as he was known then) seen Mono Lake when he was in a happier frame of mind, he might have written a glowing account of its beautiful sunsets; its pastel colors softening the landscape; of the white and black islands nestled in its bosom; in fact, a land of enchantment and adventure.

Mono Lake was and is a land of contrasts and mirages, a creature of moods, having dull listless gray days, then sparkling days of sunlit dancing water; days of low hanging fog and mist; days so clear and bright that a magnificent panorama of the views of nature that surround it are reflected on its surface.

It is often referred to as "The Dead Sea of America." It has one particular characteristic. It always appears to be close, although it may be a distance of anywhere from ten to twenty miles away. It is of glacial origin and covers an area of approximately 100 square miles in the central part of Mono County.

In the West, the Sierra peaks rise to a height of around 12,000 feet. On the South are more than twenty volcanic cones called the Mono Craters.

Further on in a distance to the east can be seen the picturesque White Mountain Range and to the north, a barren plain covered with sagebrush.

In 1879, before the railroad to Mono Mills was built, J. S. Cain of Bodie bought the Steamer Rocket and scow, a 5-ton craft which had been plying the waters of San Francisco Bay. He had it brought to

Mono Lake

Mono Craters

Sea Gulls on Negit Island, Mono Lake

Mono Lake to transfer wood and lumber from Lee Vining Creek, on the south side of the Lake across to Warford Springs. From here, its cargo was hauled to Bodie by team.

How the Steamer Rocket once took a load of panicky Chinese to refuge on Paoha Island is told elsewhere in this book.

The Rocket had a licensed pilot and was used as an excursion craft on Sundays for people who wanted to visit the islands.

The region was of great economic value to the Piutes, which is told at length in another chapter.

The Lake produced a small briny shrimp for food called by the Indians "Koo-cha-bee."

The craters furnished a fine grade of obsidian for making arrow heads. These products were bartered with other tribes.

The Lake water is heavy with minerals—sodium chloride, sodium sulphate, sodium carbonate, silica, magnesium, potassium chloride, salt, borax, and many others.

The water is a good detergent. There is no fish life.

The black island in the middle of the Lake is called Negit, which was formed by an old volcanic crater. It is a sea gull rookery and, as such, is protected by the State.

The white island, Paoha, which is two miles long and one mile wide, has springs of hot and cold water and was, in part, homesteaded by the Wallis D. McPherson family after the turn of the century. They built a seven room home here and raised fancy Toggenberg Goats. They later built Mono Inn.

A list of many of the early families who settled at Mono Lake follows: DeChambeau, Silvester, Curry, LaBraque, Thompson, Dondero, Scanovino, several Mattly families, Nay, three Farrington families, McKnight, Miller, Al Rule, and Jack Hammond, who started a store.

Stock raising and farming were the main occupations.

The streams that feed Mono Lake are being diverted into the waters taken to Los Angeles. The Lake is receding slowly as attested by its shore line. At some far distant time, it will be not a lake, but a huge saline deposit; then and only then will it become the "Solemn, Silent, Sailless Sea" as described by Mark Twain.

CHAPTER TEN

Customs and Stories of the Piute Indians

Little seems to have been written by authorities on ethnology about the powerful tribe of Indians East of the Sierra Nevada.

These were the Piutes, meaning the *Water Utes* or those who lived near the lakes and rivers in contrast to the Utes who lived in the dry region of Utah and adjoining territory.

Linguistally they spoke the Shoshone language. In our particular locality they were known as the Monos, the name meaning *beautiful* which Piute name they themselves gave to the region.

L. H. Bunnel, who was one of the discoverers of Yosemite Valley wrote: "The Monos are possessed of fine physique and have great skill in fashioning the bow and arrow."

So expert did the Monos become in making arrow heads, spears, knives, etc., from fine obsidian obtained from the Mono Craters, that all the other tribes of Indians bartered to get them.

These articles were shaped by chipping off small flakes from thin pieces of obsidian, using a deer antler for a tool and a granite boulder for a work bench. These granite boulders now called "Arrow Head Rocks" are to be found in different places in Mono County. By digging a little below the surface of the ground, fragments of obsidian and broken parts of arrow heads can be found.

The Monos had prowess in running, jumping, etc., and up to the present time they carry off many honors in athletic contests in our schools.

However, historians do not credit them with having a high order of intelligence. Their vocabulary is limited to around one thousand words.

Gesso—Bodie piute

The Piutes of Mono were not a warlike tribe and from the very first were not antagonistic to the White men who intruded upon their sanctuary. In fact, according to the early settlers, they left their usual places of habitation on the coming of the "pale faces" and went back into the deep recesses of the mountains.

Teha—104 years old

There were some few outbreaks of hostilities in the southern end of the county around Benton. Black Taylor, partner of William Bodey who discovered Bodie, was attacked in his cabin at Benton during the night and killed by savage Indians.

Captain John was the leader of the Mono County Indians.

The Piutes clothed themselves in heavy furs, deer skins, and rabbit skin blankets during the winter.

In summer the men's attire consisted of only a loin cloth. The women wore deer skin skirts or sometimes skirts made of bitter brush bark. The children for the most part were naked.

Stones and baskets used in cooking (Hot stone boiling)

The winter homes called wikiups or tonees were built like teepees, covered with skins and bark, with dirt piled around the bottom. There was one opening at the top and one large round room with a fire burning in the center. The smoke went out through the hole in the top of the room.

The Indians wrapped themselves in rabbit skin blankets at night and slept with their feet to the fire like spokes in a wheel.

In summer, they lived mostly in the open.

For their pow-wows and ceremonial occasions they used many head dresses and ornaments made of feathers and wampum beads.

Moccasins were made of the skins of animals and sewed with bone needles and buckskin thongs. These had very little ornamentation such as beads, until after the coming of the white man.

They sometimes wore as a head covering a pot shaped woven basket.

Most of their faces were painted in gay stripes and colors and occasionally with somber black stripes. The pigments were taken from the rocks and plants.

The black was indelible.

Alice, daughter of Bridgeport Tom, told the author that when Tom married her mother, he tatooed her face with a bone needle using green leaf and charcoal so that all members of the tribe would know she belonged to him. She bore the marks until she died.

The Piutes had a stone and basket age during which these articles were their only objects of utility in the home.

The flat rocks (ma-h-te) were used in different ways for rolling, kneading, grinding, and, when heated, for cooking.

The pah-ha or deeper stone bowls were used with a stone pestle (pah-ha-gu-nu) for heavier and deeper grinding.

Hot stone boiling in the making of pine nut soup, acorn mush, etc., was accomplished by taking round rocks, about as big as a tea cup, heating them in an open fire, and then depositing them in a basket filled with the mushy food to be cooked. The rocks were manipulated by means of willow sticks which had been water soaked, heated, and gradually formed into a loop.

The job of hot stone boiling was generally given to an aged woman who would sit by the camp fire for hours changing the rocks back and forth until at last the mess was cooked.

It was also the responsibility of the aged to keep the coals alive at all times, as it was no easy task to get a new spark by striking stones together.

The coals were covered by earth at night.

If the family was migrating, it was grandmother's task to carry fire. She was given a long, thick-coiled rope of bitter brush bark which was burning slowly at one end. As she walked she had to keep the fire at this end of the coil alive by blowing on it frequently.

The Indian woman was the beast of burden. It was she who had to carry the loads; the baskets filled with grains and nuts; the long pole contrivance for dragging the heavy loads behind her. Also it was her responsibility to gather, store, and provide the food for the family. The men of the tribe providing only the meat and fish.

Hers was a great worry if the food should run short in the winter —which it often did.

The Piutes had *one secret on which they were adamant.* They *never* were known to divulge their Indian names to the white man. Instead, the father of the Indian family took the given name of the white settler for whom he worked. If he worked for Dick Watkins he called himself Dick.

His wife would be Annie Dick—his children would be Sarah Dick, Emery Dick, Streeter Dick, Minnie Dick, etc. Many descendants of the Dick family still live in Bridgeport and Coleville.

We still find in Mono County large families of The James, The Toms, The Harrys, The Charlies, The Sams, and The Johns.

Sometimes they would be named as to their preference for certain things.

Big Whiskey—his son Little Whiskey. Big Coffee. Little Coffee. The Cornbreads. Matchie (who always asked for matches). Poker Bill, son Fat Bill.

While the Piutes were unmoral, and no doubt promiscuous in their relations, they must have maintained some semblance of family unity, as an old Indian being questioned as to when some event had happened will say "me father, him father, him father" meaning three generations ago.

The Piutes were very superstitious and their belief in witchcraft was general.

Years ago we took an Indian girl to a celebration at Mono Lake on Mark Twain Day. Some time after arriving, we found her covered up, head down in the back seat of the car. Thinking she was ill, we questioned her and she finally admitted an Indian woman in the crowd was trying to "witch" her and the only way she could keep from coming under her spell was to cover up her head and "no lookem."

It has often been said that the Piutes often put the so-called "witches" to death by stoning and other means, but on this subject they will not talk to the white man, being superstitious that in some way their knowledge, if divulged, will lead to bad luck for themselves.

A person who developed unusual powers for good, might be forced to become a medicine man.

If a medicine man had, unfortunately, a number of people die who were under his care, he was in disrepute and in danger of being put to death himself. He, in this case, was accused of using his powers for evil instead of good and was termed a "witch doctor."

When the first white men came into the Yosemite Valley, they found a hostile tribe, the Awahnees, entrenched in the valley, particularly in the upper part where the natural caves gave them shelter.

After some serious encounters, the Awahnees fled over the mountains and were pursued by a possee lead by Captain Sergent. They were overtaken at Lake Tenaya where their Indian Chief, Tenaya, was killed. The whites returned to the Valley, but the terrified Awahnees came across the mountains and sought refuge with the Piutes in the Mono Lake Basin.

The Monos befriended them giving them food and shelter during the winter. In the spring the Awahnees repaid them by steathily leaving during the night, stealing the Monos horses, blankets, and supplies, and starting back over the Sierras.

The Monos overtook them at a low pass in the mountains above Walker Lake and annihilated them almost to a man. From that time on, the pass has been known as Bloody Canyon.

The Awahanees being out of the way, many Mono Piutes migrated into the Yosemite Valley and made it their home, living at The Indian Village.

The Piutes were religionists who prayed to "the-one-who-was-here-before-I-came." They believed they drew their power from inanimate objects of nature around them.

If one found his power to be in the rocks—or the winds—or the clouds, he prayed to that diety to help him in his undertakings. He did nothing without consulting the source of his power. If his power were used for evil, he might be in danger of being put to death.

Photo compliments of Yosemite Museum

The last of the Yosemite Awahnees who escaped the Mono Slaughter

The Piutes believed implicitly in the tradition of the flood, almost parallel to the Christian belief, and would point to the marks on the mountains where the water had receded.

The night before a burial, the Monos even now often hold a cry dance and the Indians come from long distances to attend. They sit in a large circle, swaying back and forth and emitting dismal crys of mourning, the object being to get the ghost of the departed to go away and to start on his journey to "the happy hunting grounds." Always the belongings of the deceased will be burned in an open bonfire in front of the mourners, and blankets, baskets, etc., will be thrown on the blaze as a sacrificial offering to the powers that be.

A widow may call her friends to a second cry dance for her deceased husband. During the crying ceremony she will remove the signs of mourning (black streaks) from her face. Her hair which has been cut short will in the future be allowed to grow, thus signifying that her term of mourning is over. At *this,* cry dance articles of the family and other tokens may be burned; but this is not deemed necessary.

Their burial customs were closely guarded secrets as were also the places of burial.

At one time in Aurora, my husband and I were awakened at night by the tramp of horses going by. On looking out, we saw a long line of Indians on horseback and in the middle of the procession was a horse being led, carrying a prone figure of an adult wrapped in a blanket and strapped across its back, head dangling on one side and feet on the other.

It was a silent procession in the moonlight, not a sound except the beating of hoofs on the ground.

Some time afterward an old Mahala (Indian woman) who had worked for us for many years and trusted us, told us a young man had died. They were taking his remains to one of the highest peaks around and had buried him in the rocks where the wind could blow through. She explained that he had prayed to the winds and they would be kind to him and take him to "happy hunting grounds."

A short time ago a notice appeared in the Inyo County *Register* stating that an Indian resident of the Indian village in Bishop had died. His friends were invited to attend a cry dance the night before burial which would be in the Pioneer Cemetery in Bishop. Religious services were to be held the morning of the funeral in a Christian Church in town.

Old Jennie Piute had worked for Mrs. David Hays for years around the house. Bob, her husband, helped around the store, yard, and barn. Bob accidentally caught his arm in a separator and was terribly mangled. Dr. Cushman operated on Bob in the David Hays' wash house, cutting off the mangled arm. Bob died. Old Jennie was broken hearted. She put on the usual widow's sign of mourning, black painted face, and cut short her hair.

Supposedly all of Bob's worldly effects had been burned at the cry dance or buried with him. Still Bob's ghost kept coming back to Jennie at night, hand out-stretched. Jennie could not sleep. She was worried. She finally confided her trouble to Mrs. Hays. Bob wanted something, which evidently had not been burned or buried with him. An old pair of overalls was found hanging in the barn. These were given to Jennie to be burned. Still Bob kept coming. Then an old battered hat, a pair of shoe strings, a group photo, in which Bob was in the background, were consigned to the flames, but still Bob appeared each night.

Poor old Jennie could neither eat nor sleep, knowing Bob was so unhappy. One day on a dark shelf in the wash room she found Bob's old corn cob pipe with the tobacco half smoked. That night she burned it. Bob appeared no more. "Bob heap likum that pipe," Jennie told Mrs. Hays.

Around 1915 while living in Aurora, Nevada, the writer had an experience which was baffling, but the next day the explanation of it seemed quite simple.

Our old Mahala, Susie, failed to come to work one morning and, as she was usually so punctual, I walked some distance up to the Piute camps to find out the reason for her non-appearance.

Old Susie was sitting, apparently alone, at the camp on the edge of a blanket that was spread out flat on the ground, and anchored by rocks. When I approached, she started to wave her hands wildly and say *"You go home—go home."* Her tone was mandatory and thinking she had been greatly offended by something I had done, I turned and started down the hill. As I did, I heard a sound like a moan and looking back I saw only old Susie sitting there straight and still. I was more mystified than ever.

Her story next day was this.

To hasten a difficult birth of a baby, a trench was dug in the earth for the expectant mother. A fire was built in the excavation and the ground heated. The fire was then pulled out and the pregnant woman put down in the hot earth. This no doubt expedited to a great extent the delivery of the baby.

Old Susie had been acting in the capacity of mid-wife and did not want *me* to interfere with her duties.

FOOD OF THE PIUTES

The pine nut was the Mono's main article of food.

(This is not to be confused with the pinon nut of Mexico which is very much smaller and not so mealy.)

From the pine nuts, the Piutes made soup, mush, and bread (the dried nuts would last from one year to the next and were ground into flour). This nut was bartered with the "Diggers" (Miwoks) for acorns which grew only on the west slope of the Sierra Nevada. The Indians depended a great deal on the acorns for food.

Sarah Dick Gracian, an aged Piute woman still living in Bridgeport, is my authority for some of the following foods used by her people before the coming of the white man.

A mealy potato, ko-ge-ha, which grew at the roots of the Mariposa Lily, found around what is now the Ranger Station near Bridgeport.

Pine nuts
Wild onions
Rose buds
Wild rhubarb (which grew in Slinkard Canyon above Coleville)
Taboose, a tuber—sweet and milky
Huki seeds for seasoning
Sweet grass seeds
Tule roots and roots of California Bulrush and swamp grass—boiled down and used for sweetening (Pra-ba)
Wild mountain rice (Wai)
June bugs, chipmunks, squirrels, locust
Elder berries
Tom cat clover
Wild currants
Choke cherries
Buck berries—very tart
Squaw cabbage (greens)
Rabbits
Deer and Antelope—(Antelope Valley was former name of Coleville)
Gophers (Ku be)
Porcupines
Ground hogs

Sarah Dick Gracian, authority on food of the Piutes

Lizards
Quail
Grouse
Sage hen
Mountain Sheep
Ducks, Geese and a variety of other edible birds.
Salt (scraped from alkali marshes)
Pe-agge (caterpillars from the pine tree)
Ko-cha-bee (Mono Lake worms)
Waya (rye grass seeds)
Sun flower seeds (dried and ground into meal)
Jerkie (over supply of meat dried in long strings and stored away)
Seeds were stored in grass lined pits
Chubs and suckers—(which they speared or netted or caught on bone hooks)
(The white settlers planted trout and carp in the lakes and streams)

The Indians did not eat the coyote as it was, according to their tradition, the "Spirit of Evil."

The Wolf—"Spirit of Good" also was not eaten.

Wild parsnips were a deadly poison, eaten only when a person wanted to commit suicide.

The Piutes seemed to have used few medicines. Squaw tea—su-du-pe—was a panacea for every ailment. It was made by boiling the long, jointed spikes of the "squaw tea" bush and drinking the tea or applying it locally to any afflicted part. The medicine man allowed the use of su-du-pe.

For the housewife of today who can buy a loaf of bread from a grocery shelf, I will endeavor to trace the slow and laborious process of an Indian woman making acorn bread.

The woman, being a Mono, has perhaps spent many long days in carrying the acorns from the western slope of the mountains in a huge burden basket.

The next day she seeks the shade of a tree, if there happens to be one near, and the process of making bread begins.

She places the acorns in her grinding bowl, hewn out of stone. Slowly she raises the huge stone pestle and pounds down the acorns

Piute with burden basket

in the bowl. She repeats this process many times, as she sifts the fine meal through a fan-shaped basket and again pounds the coarser stuff. The fan shaped basket also serves as a winnower, as the outer section of the acorn drops off with the sifting.

The meal now has a bitter strong taste, probably caused by the outer part of the acorn. It is then mixed with water and lye (the latter being made from wood ashes) and thrown into a large, coarsely woven, pot shaped basket through which the moisture seeps away.

When it is in the form of a paste, it is cut into short strips and put out into the sun to dry; but this is not the finished product as you might think.

It is again pounded into meal, and mixed with water and put into a basket where it is subjected to the hot stone boiling process (described elsewhere). Here it assumes the consistancy of a thick glutinous mush and may be eaten as such. If it is to be in the form of bread, the mush is again dried, again pounded, and mixed with water. Then it is pressed into small cakes, and baked on a heated flat stone. This finished acorn bread product was one of the Mono's chief article of diet.

The Monos had three big festivals or pow-wows during the year, held when the pine nuts, the ko-cha-bee, and pe-agg-e crops were harvested.

The pine nut crop would be plentiful in some districts, say around Benton, while there would not be any crop on the trees in another section.

The Piutes would scout around to find the best place to "pine nut" and a general migration would take place to that point.

Whole villages would spring up in the nut section over night.

Camp fires would light up the horizon and excitement filled the air.

If perchance there had been a heavy frost, the burs would burst open on the trees and the nuts would fall to the ground. In this case it was a race between the squirrels and Indians to gather the nuts first.

If a frost did not come to lighten the harvesting, the burs were pulled off the trees by means of long wooden poles with hooks fashioned at the ends. The burs were then thrown into a deep pit in the ground which had been pre-heated by fire. When the heat opened the burs, the nuts were easily shaken or beaten out.

They were then placed in a winnowing, fan-shaped basket and shaken in the wind. The empty shells blew away. If the nuts were to be eaten at once, they were then roasted.

Most of the pe-agge or caterpillar worms were harvested at Mono Mills or east of the Mono Craters.

Their home is the Jeffery pine.

This delicacy is the larva of the Pandora moth. Hatching generally occurs in August. The young caterpillars feed on the tree for about two months, then they gather in clusters on the higher branches. Here they remain dormant for the winter. When spring comes they continue to grow until they are from two to three inches long.

The Indians used to dig a trench circling the outside of the tree. It was about twelve inches deep and fifteen inches wide, the outside wall being verticle. The caterpillars dropped off the tree and fell, or eventually crawled, into this trench where they were harvested.

Sometimes the harvesting was speeded up by a fire "with heap smoke," being built under the tree.

The pe-agg-e was then roasted with coals in a mound of earth. The dirt, when allowed to cool, was sifted out and the worms stored away for future use. As much as a ton of these caterpillars have been taken at a single harvesting.

The ko-cha-bee is a small Mono Lake worm in a shell, which on coming to the surface will soon burst its shell and become a fly. (It is the larva of the Ephydna-hyana).

The small shells are driven ashore by the tide and form a border from two to three feet wide, around the shore of the Lake. Here they were scooped up by the Indian women in winnowing baskets.

They were dried in the sun and the shells rubbed off, leaving a small yellow worm.

These were considered to be the greatest delicacy of the Piute world.

They were hung in sacks in the wikiups or campoodies and did not smell unlike a shrimp. A real test of an Indian's friendship for you was for him or her to offer you a piece of pine nut or acorn bread sprinkled with ko-cha-bee.

This food was held in such high regard by the Monos that worm claims were staked out around the shore of the Lake, generally by the Captain of the tribe, and warfare ensued if one group infringed upon the worm claim of another.

Gambling games, played with sticks for counters, singing and dancing were in progress during the nights of each harvesting. The campfires lighted up the scene for many miles around and "pale white faces" often watched and listened from a distance as the dancing, singing figures were silhouetted against the horizon.

Each festival or pow-wow of course was held at the scene of the harvesting; the ko-cha-bee festival at Mono Lake being the biggest. Here the Piutes would congregate from great distances and the pow-wow would last for a week or more. For the night celebrations, the Monos wore their ceremonial dress, war bonnets, feathers, and deer skin clothing.

At the beating of the tom-toms, the dancers would form in a circle around the camp fire—arms folded and figures swaying from side to side, at first uttering only gutteral sounds. As the crescendo increased, the chanting at times took on a war-like tone and the participants worked themselves into a sort of a frenzy. (In the days before the coming of the white men, the Indians were not known to have had any intoxicants; but later the white man's "fire water" provided fuel to the flame.)

Always during the harvestings, the gambling games played with bones and sticks were in progress.

The players divided into two groups sitting opposite each other with blankets spread over their laps. The wampum (money) for which they played was put out of reach in a hole in the ground. Two sticks were given each side to be used as counters. One group took two small bones and putting their hands under the blanket began singing and swaying from side to side, the object being to stealthily hide the two bones in the hands of one of their players; the opposite side having to guess in which player's hands the bones were hidden. If they did guess, the bones and one of the sticks used as counters

Part of the author's collection of Indian Baskets

were thrown over to the successful guessers. The side who had all four of the counting sticks first, won the game.

The gambling instinct was strong in the Indians, particularly in the men. Young boys were taught to gamble.

A story was told at Mono Mills, long ago, that a father losing all his possessions, in desperation, finally put his very young daughter in pawn, to a man three times her age, lost again, and the crying girl was taken away by the winner.

The squaws also were gamblers and played in games by themselves or with the bucks. The terms "squaws" and "bucks" are considered to be terms of derision by the Indians.

PIUTE BASKETRY

Baskets were the most highly prized possession of the Piutes. They were their wherewithals, their everything. Without them their mode of existence, however primitive, could not have been maintained.

Baskets were used for the cooking of food; for the carrying and storing of water (when pitched); for dishes with which to eat and to hold food; for the scooping up of seeds and nuts, and grains; for

Indian water jugs

slacking acorns; for winnowing; for carrying their burdens; as cradles for their babies; for headwear; for the storing of food; and lastly (the most beautiful examples of their artistic ability) for treasure recepticles for their valued wampum and beads.

The ingenuity which the Indian women displayed in making these baskets is astonishing.

Great thought must have gone into the construction and shape so that the basket would function for the need of the user.

For instance, a woven pitched water jub, (o-sa-h) if intended for desert use when water was being carried long distances, had a pointed bottom so the burden could be laid down at times and the water would not pour out. If, however, the o-sa-h was made for home use the bottom was flat so that it would stand upright on a table.

Winnowing baskets

The water jugs were made water tight by putting hunks of pitch from the pine tree into the jug and shaking it around with hot pebbles which dissolved the pitch. Hot pitch was also smeared on the outside. These water tight o-sa-h's were made in all sizes from large to small.

The winnowing baskets were flat, fan-shaped, and closely woven. The Indian woman would shake the nuts, grains, or seeds up and down. If the shells were empty, they would blow away. The grains or seeds would give up the chaff.

For cleaning pine nuts, to get rid of the long pine needles that were gathered with them, a basket similar to the winnower was made, but the spaces beween the weaving were long and narrow so that the pine needles would drop through to the ground.

The burden baskets were constructed like hollow cones, most of them large. They were carried on the back if the burden was heavy. A wide, flat piece of leather attached to the basket was placed around the forehead and the point of the burden baskets rested on the small of the back. Hence the weight of the load was distributed. Other burden baskets were smaller and carried in the arms.

If the burden baskets were used for carrying pine cones, they

Hoopa *or baby basket*

were loosely woven, and light in weight. If, however, they were to be used for grains or seeds, they were closely constructed and generally had very beautiful designs woven into them.

The baby baskets (hoo-pa) were made by the grandmother before the child was born. However, the design on the head shade was not put on until *after* the birth of the baby. This design denoted the sex of the child in the basket. If a boy (nat-se), the design was a straight line or arrow; if a girl (tse-u-za), the design was a diamond.

The beautiful, artistic baskets made by the Mono weavers were among the finest to be found anywhere in the United States.

The Monos lived in such an isolated region that their fine basketry was little known or appreciated until it was too late.

It was hard to believe in looking at one of these primitive women that she had the creative ability of a real artist.

The Indian woman had to gather materials from nature, and prepare her materials for making baskets.

The twig of the willow was the most used material. All utility baskets around the home were woven of willow. It was worked down to the size of a coarse flat string by scraping it with a piece of sharp obsidian. Then in the weaving, it was pulled through the lips to find the rough and uneven places. The writer has often seen the basket weaver with a bleeding mouth.

When Indian Field Day was instituted in the Yosemite Valley for a few years around 1925-1929, and contests in basketry were held; baskets that were breath taking in their beauty of design, size and coloring were exhibited by the Mono weavers.

Into her baskets each weaver had expressed the art that filled her soul. They were her music, her appreciation of the beauties of nature, her means of depicting the legends of her race. Here you could discern the mountains, the water falls, the trees, the medicine men, the hunters, the rivers, the flowers, the birds, the diamond-back rattlesnake.

The last-named was a favorite design as it was a prayer of appeasement to the powers that controlled the rattlesnake (which abounded in the region) that the weaver's family would not be bitten as they wandered in the snake-infested districts.

Sally Sam weaving a basket

Indian Field Day in Yosemite, 1926

The writer, being a collector of Indian baskets for over forty years, could go on indefinitely, dear reader, telling you of the lore and legends woven into these baskets; but, being afraid of boring you, will instead show you a few pictures in this chapter.

For the fine artistic baskets, fern or grass root was generally used for the body. This made them rather varigated and darker than the willow baskets. The designs were woven with cats-claw fern (black) and the strippings of the wild rose bush (red). The two colors were generally used on the same basket to make the design stand out. The colors in these baskets never faded.

The basket weaver in her own calculable way had preconceived the size and design of the basket she intended making, but at no time used a drawing or pattern before her. An onlooker would have no idea, even when the basket was half completed, of what the finished product would be like. The designs were put on with a precision and repetition that was absolutely accurate.

After the Monos had practically wiped out the Awahanee tribe at the battle of Bloody Canyon (told elsewhere), many Mono Piutes took up their homes in the Yosemite Valley and most of them became famous, being written up in numerous articles and magazines.

The most noted was Maggie Howard, who became a narrator of Indian Lore and was known as "The Historian of the Piute Tribe." She had previously been married to Jack Lundy of Bridgeport and was the mother of Sim Lundy (expert arrowhead maker) still living. Her interviews appeared often in current papers and magazines under the Indian name of "Taboose."

Lucy Tom Telles, daughter of Bridgeport Tom, was a weaver of fine beautiful baskets. She exhibited her work and did weaving at Treasure Island during the Panama Pacific International Exposition (PPIE).

Her sister, Alice James Wilson, was also an expert basket weaver and was employed for years at the gift shop at the Awahanee Hotel in Yosemite Valley, demonstrating to the tourists the art of weaving and beading baskets.

Other fine basket weavers were Carrie Bethel, Nellie Jameson, Maria Harry, Tillie Young Charlie, Teena Young Charlie, Rosie August, Minnie Brown.

Harry Tom of Mono Lake was a noted athlete in running, jumping, and swimming.

The Mono weaver would always tell you "black root—cats-claw-fern cost heap much" as it did not grow on the eastern slope of the mountain and had to be bartered with the "Diggers."

The writer bought a basket from Tillie Young Charlie having a design of all black which covered half or more of the basket. The maker explained that it was a mourning basket and she had put rain, wind, thunder, lightening, and everything bad on the basket because the white man had forced her son to fight his war (World War I).

The baskets exhibited on Indian Field Day in the Yosemite Valley, especially those taking the best prizes, were quickly bought from the maker at worthwhile prices.

The rules of the Committee were these:

1st—The maker must exhibit her own basket.

2nd—She must still own it.

Alice James Wilson of Mono Lake holding up a prize basket at the opening of Awahanee Hotel

3rd—It must have been made within the year.

When Yosemite Field Day was discontinued, the Mono basket-maker lost her incentive for making these wonderful three coil baskets as there was no competition for prizes and awards with other good basket makers.

Fewer and fewer worthwhile baskets were made as the years went by, until now Mono Basketry is practically a lost art.

The younger generation will give neither the time nor the patience of weeks and months in the development of a single basket. The white man's money can be had much more quickly by working at menial tasks.

If a buyer of baskets went to the homes of the Indian women, which were generally in the Mono Lake district, it was a long and drawn out process to even get a weaver to *show* her basket. She would come to the opening or door of her dwelling in response to your knock, shut the door behind her, and never speak.

Invariably the following dialogue would ensue:

Buyer—"Me come to see you basket."

Mahala—"Me no gottum."

Buyer—"Yes you gottum."

Mahala—"How you know?"

Buyer—"Somebody tell me."

Mahala—"How he know?"*

Buyer—"He see you makem."

Mahala—"Who tell you?"

Buyer—"Somebody."

Mahala—"What he say?"

Buyer—"He say you long time sittum down makem good basket."

Mahala—"How long?"

Buyer—"He don't tellem me."

Mahala—"What for he talk about my work?"

Buyer—"He say me come and see *good* work, you makem *good work.*"

Mahala—"Maybe you laugh my work."

Buyer—"No I no laugh you work. I know you makem good work,

*Indians use only masculine gender

you go gettum."

Reluctantly she turns, enters the hut, and brings out her basket which is generally in a flour sack. She unties the sack slowly, pulls out the basket and offers it to you in an apologetic way. You take it without comment and turn it around. She watches you, studying your face.

Knowing what constitutes a good basket you look for these characteristics:

1st—It must be perfect and pleasing in design.

2nd—Symmetrical in shape.

3rd—Uniform in stitch.

4th—Pleasing in color.

5th—Smooth on the inside.

If there are imperfections, you do not speak of them. The maker knows her mistakes better than you do.

If the basket is a perfect or more nearly perfect specimen, do not be afraid to praise it. It will not cost you any more to do so; perhaps less.

If you decide to buy, which most generally is at the maker's price, she still shows a feeling of reluctance at selling her treasure, her artistic masterpiece. You carry it away regretting the fact that perhaps her necessity has made her part with it.

Indian baskets are gradually finding their way into museums all over the United States. The old utility baskets which used to contain food, water, babies, and had a hundred uses in the Indian home, are now the antiques of the Indian world.

In 1905 when many Indians worked at the Mono Mills Lumber Camp, E. W. Billeb, then Superintendent, sent for a shipment of fine Indian seed beads which were, and still are, imported from Czechoslovakia.

He encouraged the Indian women living there to make a beaded basket by covering with beads the outside of the woven willow basket.

The Indian women worked for months trying to develop the beaded basket as the process of putting on the design in beads was just the opposite of weaving the design in a willow basket. That is, the starting and ending points were reversed. In the beaded basket,

Governor Richardson awarding prizes to Mono County basket makers in Yosemite Valley, 1929

the starting point had to be at the top of the willow basket in order to get a purchase for the beads. The design ended in the center bottom of the willow foundation basket.

If, when the beaded basket was finished, the design in the bottom center was not perfect, the basket was a failure. Then the maker pulled the beads off and the process started anew. This happened not once but probably several times until the finished product was perfect. These beaded baskets were artistically beautiful both in design and coloring. The art of making them spread into the adjacent territory of Nevada, but the work made there did not compare with that done in Mono County.

The development of the beaded basket was so slow and complicated, and the beads so expensive, that probably not more than a few hundred were made.

I know of only one good maker of beaded baskets who is still interested in her art. She is Carrie McGowan Bethel of Lee Vining, California. Her baskets are treasures.

Mono County can well be proud of the outstanding contribution of her Piute Indian women to the *one true* art of America, which fast is becoming a lost art.

CHAPTER ELEVEN

The Story of Captain John

This is the story of an Indian Chief, who was for many years absolute ruler of a thousand subjects in the Mono Area. Owing to the disobedience of his people to his last, and most important, edict, he proclaimed that he was no longer their Chief and leader, and died a few years later a broken hearted and lonely old man.

Captain John of The Mono Piutes was a person, I, the writer, had long waited to meet. I had entertained visions of him as a potentate—surrounded by his subjects, living in a sort of Utopia near the shores of Mono Lake. I was quite disillusioned, however, with his surroundings on our visit to him, but it *was* and *is* a never-to-be-forgotten memory.

My husband, who had known John for some years, finally consented to take me by buggy team, over what he knew would be rough and hazardous roads, to the place where John lived in the Mono Basin.

We had gone many miles too far when we were finally directed by a rancher to go back until we came to a divide where we were to branch off the main road. This we found and followed along a sandy creek bed to a place known as the Patroli ranch on the north side of Mono Lake.

Stopping at this ranch, we saw a small barefooted Italian boy peeking at us from behind a tree. My husband held up a coin and the boy's fear suddenly left him and he came up to the buggy. In answer to our question, he directed us to continue on over a road mostly overgrown with sagebrush. Pointing to a place where a faint outline of smoke was rising in the distance, he said "John lives down there, but why you wanta see that Indian Wop? Maybe you better notta go. All Indians and some white men are afraid of thata John. You know what some people call him?" Here he put his hand partly over his mouth and whispered, "A Witch Man."

Captain John's home on the north side of Mono Lake

We rode at least two miles further over a still more bumpy and sagebrush road. As we drew closer to the little settlement where John lived, we could see a number of his children and wives moving about.

There were three wikiups and some tonees (Indian houses) but no trees, no vegetation; nothing but scrubby sagebrush.

The day being clear, we could look across the glistening waters of Mono Lake to the mountains in the distance.

John was sitting in the sun near the doorway of the largest wikiup of his tonee. All other persons had disappeared on our approach. He came forward as we dismounted from the buggy and recognizing my husband, he put up his hand to him and then to me as a gesture of friendliness. Had he not been glad to see us, I learned later, he would have folded his hands behind his back.

He was a stockily built, square shouldered man probably around sixty years of age. He had the high cheek bones and wide nose characteristic of his race. His eyes were cunning and piercing and seemed to fathom your innermost thoughts. The words "Witch Man" came to me, but I quickly tried to put them out of my mind.

He had on an Army coat of the Spanish American War, a pair of trousers tucked into high boots which had probably come from the same source as the coat.

My husband had brought him some packages of shotgun shells, which seemd to please him greatly, and taking the shells he said in good English "Thank you, young Cain." There was a pause of several minutes, a most embarrassing pause, for John was waiting, in true Indian fashion, for us to tell him why we had come. (A social visit was something he would not understand.) If we had come to bring the cartridges, why didn't we go?

Quite apologetically, my husband then explained that for a long time I had wanted to see the Captain of the Piute Tribe and talk with him. Here John gave a sort of a grunt and a sarcastic smile played about his mouth.

"Indian got nothing to say that white man want to hear," he said, "Indian just have to listen and do what white man tell 'em, that's all." Another pause.

Then my husband asked him if we could tie up the horses for a little while and rest before starting back to Bodie.

He led the team to the hitching post and tied them, then without a word walked before us to the large opening before his wikiup. Logs had been cut in cross sections, the height of a stool, and were placed so that they formed a circle around the opening. There were evidences of fires having been built in the center.

I suddenly realized this was John's court, the council place of the leaders of the tribe when they met with their Chief.

John seated himself and then motioned us to sit near him.

"Now what you want to know?" he said, addressing me. I told him I had been teaching school in Bodie before I married "young Cain," that I was very much interested in the Indians and their history and how the coming of the white man had changed their lives. Inadvertently, I had touched off the spark of a long slumbering flame.

"Yes, white man change everything for red man," he said, "That is why Captain John live on sagebrush land, hear no running water, have no trees where birds can sing. John born over there," he said, pointing to the Silver Lake country. "Indian then know where to get everything Indian need. We happy people. We hear from Indian runners about white man coming into Big Meadows (Bridgeport Valley). Indians all heap afraid but man no hurt them. Give them hogadi (food) and show them to fire what they call guns to kill birds and animals. Something tell John inside here (pointing to his head) that white man no good for Indian but we wait and see.

"Some time we see white man in Mono Lake country, but they stay more on side of mountains in Big Meadows where grass grow good. They make boards out of trees and put up houses.

"Piutes have big meeting when old Chief die. They make John new Chief, but I tell them get older man. They say 'Old man not good now, we need young man to talk to pale faces, young man to stand up and fight for Piute people.' They say 'You know many words now John and for long time white man say "Send John, we talk to him." '

"So John was made Captain of Piute Tribe in what we call Mono. John had three wives then and many children. We live on ground that you call Farrington ranch.

"One day two big wagons pulled by, what you call oxen, came to our place. A woman and children were inside wagon. It had big round white top and we could see blankets not made of skins and things we don't know about. The man got out and he came over with what you call paper in his hand. 'You Captain John?' he say. (That's what white man call me.) 'Well John you no can read paper, but this land belong me now. I come to live here. Government call it homestead. You move out John on other land. It is big country around here. Indian know more about getting food than white man do. You won't have hard time, John, I give you horse to help you.'

"Two days after, we carry big loads and walk long way. My children heap cry but I tell 'em we find a good place, where we can have running water.

"Then we find good place again on what you now call Mattly ranch. We stay there two winters, three summers when another white man come. He talk again much about government going to settle people on land. Tell about big white Chief in Washington and how Indian have to do what white chief say. Then he tell me Government going to give this land to him because Indian don't know how to make land grow things to eat. He tell me to stay little while longer and look around for new place. He put up fingers and tell me *that many* sleeps he come back.

"This time we move around Lake to another place but always had to get on place where we have water. Then another white man come with paper. He say same thing. This time I feel very mad inside me, but what can Indian do? Then I move over here on this sagebrush land that no white man wants. No grass, no trees, just a little water that runs down from ranch up there. Some times no water come and we have to go get it.

"Duck ponds on this side of Lake. I walk down there and bring home many ducks for my women and children to eat. I be on my belly for long time to get many with one shot. Some day I come to Bodie and bring you ducks."

He did come soon afterwards riding on an old grey horse with a gunny sack full of ducks tied behind him. He seemed pleased when we praised them as he laid them out on the porch; teals, mallards, sprig, and canvas-backs, in an array of beautiful colors—many, many more than we could use. "Young Cain" took him to the store and bought him more cartridges, groceries, and gave him some silver dollars. He held the silver dollars in his hand for a long time, looking at them thoughtfully.

Several months elapsed before we saw him again, but this time he brought no ducks. He tied up the old grey saddle horse and came slowly to the door. My husband greeted him and said "It's a stormy day for you to come to Bodie, Captain John."

"John no mind storm," he answered, "no afraid of bad weather; bad weather go way but Indian got trouble here, (pointing to his heart) that never go way."

What is it, John?" said my husband. "Tell us about it. What's your trouble?"

"Well," he said slowly, "this thing happen and I no understand. I ask you, my friend, what it mean.

"Two days ago I be for long time on my belly to get good shot at ducks. Then I bang, bang, and many birds fall dead in water. Then a hand grab me by collar from behind and pull me up quick. A man with big star on his coat say 'What are you doing there, Red Devil? Don't you know you no can shoot ducks now? I can put you in jail for doing this.' 'What you talk?' I ask him and I shake all over. 'You mean white man own all ducks, too? Indian can no more eat ducks?' 'Well, sometimes he can eat them' he say, 'but not now. Government knows how to take care of birds and fish. Indian he no understand. Government tell him when he can shoot birds and catch fish. You no more do this 'til white man tells you it's all right.' Then I tell him 'You all time say Indian no understand Government. He understand. I no savvy what you mean by Government, but I know he no good for Indian. You white man go home. Go back your own country. Give Indians back his lands, his lakes, his rivers, his birds, his fish. You steal everything from red man.'

" 'I not here to fight you, John' say man with the star. 'This my job to take care of birds and fish and you Indians do what we tell you —hear?' He walk away and I stand there long time in one place just looking at ducks on top of water. Then I go home with no meat for my wives and children to eat."

We tried to explain the logic of conservation to him, but his counter-argument was, "Why do white man come here to eat up Indian's food? Let white man go back where he come from across big water. Give Indian his country back. Always there will be plenty of fish and animals and birds for Indian to eat."

We saw him less frequently after that, perhaps because he had no offering of ducks to bring.

On his last visit to Bodie, we told him we were moving to Aurora, Nevada, a distance of about twelve miles farther away. He seemed disappointed and said, "Well, my friends, I see you some time again, but my old horse not too good any more to go long way."

Some time elapsed before we saw him again. His old grey horse was all fagged out before he reached Aurora, a distance from his home of about twenty miles. I upbraided him when I saw he was wearing spurs and said, "John, I no feed you if you stick spurs in your poor old horse." He smiled and answered, "I no kick 'em much, just little bit when I see woman coming." (He had at this time six wives and innumerable children.)

Captain John's last wife

This time he had a secret to tell my husband. He took out a specimen of rock that showed free gold and explained that many years ago, when he was a young man, he had broken off this fragment of rock one day while hunting deer. The croppings from whence it had come were some miles from Aurora toward the East.

He would show the place to "young Cain" if he wanted to go with him. Did "young Cain" want to go? Foolish question. He could hardly wait! The next day my husband rented a pack outfit from a prospector, two saddle horses and two burros, as it was an overnight trip and they had to carry supplies, blankets, and canteens of water.

They left early one morning and came back the next evening with samples from a small ledge that Captain John had had no trouble in locating.

Assays, made at the Assay Office, showed it went $78.00 a ton in gold and silver. My husband was in a high pitch of excitement and so was Captain John when he was told it was good, *heap good.*

The find was kept a deep dark secret until the claims were staked out and location notices posted. Captain John and "young Cain" made two night trips to the place, going over desert country all the way.

In true Indian fashion, John took advantage of any slight knoll or raise of ground to look back and see if they were being followed.

Location notices were filed in Hawthorne, Nevada, on "The Captain John Mining Co," and when the news leaked out, there was a mild excitement in Aurora and an exodus to the place with a number of adjoining claims being located.

"Young Cain" put two men to work on the ledge, one was a Scotch miner named Bill McRae, the other a Chinese called Ah Yang.

They were an odd pair and it wasn't long before they were at daggar's points. The only thing they had in common were "cuss words."

A Chinese boy called "China Willie" was hired to tend camp, and came to Aurora three times a week for water and supplies. McRae had two names for his helpers—"Yellow Skinned Heathens" and "Chinese Bastards."

In their native sing song language, they too were probably calling old Mac all the names in the Chinese calendar.

The ledge was followed for a couple of months, but did not widen out or improve in value. Then one day it just quit, "pinched out" as the miners say, leaving a worthless trench in the Nevada desert.

My husband was quite disappointed and when he told Captain John, who had been staying in Aurora with some Indian friends, John showed disappointment, too.

"Well, Captain," "young Cain" said, "I guess we not going to get rich like we thought." "I no want to get rich," John answered. "All I want is wagon and two horses. John getting too old to ride saddle horse. Saddle horse getting too old to carry John."

John kept hanging around Aurora for some time without any apparent reason. We saw him from time to time and he hardly spoke. Something was troubling him.

One evening about dusk, he came to our home. Would "young Cain" go with him up the mountain, he asked? He had something to say that no one else must hear.

Of course he would go, and seated on the hilltop, he poured out to my husband the most closely guarded secret of his life. It was this:

He knew the location of what was called throughout Western Nevada "The Lost Mexican Mine." It was a very rich mine, John told him, and the Mexicans used to carry the ore all the way to Sacramento on burros. When they came back, they had plenty of supplies and plenty of white man's whiskey.

They had two or three encounters with the Indians going and coming, but the Indians were always routed by the Mexican's guns. Then one night when the Mexicans were drunk and asleep, the Indians raided the camp, scalped the Mexicans, and threw them down the shaft. They poured big rocks, stones, and dirt down the hole, loaded the burros and horses with everything in camp and, giving a war-hoop, took themselves off to the hills.

The Mexican mine was never found but John's story was so minute in detail that my husband was satisfied that John had first hand information of what had happened that night long years before at "The Lost Mexican Mine."

Many prospectors have tried unsuccessfully throughout the years to locate this mine as it is a well-known fact that Mexicans *had* worked a rich mine and *had* mysteriously disappeared. A rumor persisted in Aurora that a white man had lived with a "squaw" and raised several children on the strength of her showing him The Lost Mine, (which she never did).

John broke a long silence after his story by saying, "What you think, young Cain, you like me show you that place? It long way off from Aurora near Adobe Meadows, but we maybe get there in two day, one night, by saddle horse."

"I tell you, Captain John," answered my husband, "I'll get McRae to go with you. He has more savvy about things like that than I have.

You show Mac, then we work claims like we did before on the Captain John Mining Co. Mac will have to go later anyway, so you go with him. Don't be afraid to show him. He's all right. I just tell him you want to go show him the place where Mexicans used to mine."

Two days later, John and McRae started towards Powell Mountain and the Adobe Meadows country. As they rode along in the afternoon of the first day Mac was talking too much to suit Captain John, being too inquisitive as to how much John knew about the mine, etc. Finally, John said to McRae, "What we do with Mexicans when we find 'em?" And McRae answered, "Hell! We'll dig 'em up." John looked back at him and gave a loud grunt. Then he became so sullen and silent that McRae finally got tired of the sound of his own voice and stopped talking, and the two traveled along in silence. They pitched camp that night near a spring of water with pine trees growing on the side hill. There was a full moon. John didn't speak a word but wrapped himself up in his blanket and rolled over on the ground, his back to McRae.

During the night an owl kept hooting in the pine trees. John seemed to be restless, as he kept moving around and turning over.

At sun-up, McRae cooked the breakfast, loaded the burros with all the things they had used, and saddling the horse was ready to travel on. John had eaten in silence and after saddling his horse, he turned it around to face the direction in which they had come the day before. Then he said to McRae, "I go back to Aurora today; last night Ghost Man talk."

"Ghost Man be damned," said McRae, "what kind of a Captain of the Piute Tribe are you? Go back home, you lousy old redskin. Walk around with baby on your back. Send one of your old squaws out to find a mine, she maybe not afraid of hoot owl."

John made no reply but, mounting his horse, rode all day in silence. By evening, they had reached Aurora. Of course, my husband was greatly disappointed. (John afterwards told him that he was afraid if the Mexicans were dug up, "Ghost Man" would bring bad luck to some Indians still living.)

When the Captain went back to Mono Lake, he was driving an old wagon and two horses and was greatly pleased.

Captain John

Months passed and one day there stood John at the door. "Hello, Captain, I am glad to see you again; come right in," "young Cain" said in a cheery voice. He answered sadly, "You no more call me Captain, call me *John, just John.* I no more Captain of Piute Indians of Mono County, *no more Captain.*"

"Why, John, what has happened? Tell us."

Seating himself, he waited, as was his custom, for some minutes before he began. "Well, you know, my friends, of big war between white people of this land and white people of other lands across big ocean." (World War I.) "Some time ago white man with paper come among my people. He ask many questions about Indian boys, when born, who was Mother and Father, and he write what they say on paper. Then he tell them, 'maybe you have to go to war for this country and help us fight.' When I hear this, I jump up quick. 'Why you ask Indian boys go fight for this Government?' I tell my boys '*You no go—you stay here*—Government no do anything for Indians, just take everything away, give nothing back to Indians.' He say, 'John, you no raise trouble, we put you in jail, keep you there long time—maybe till war is over.' And I say, 'You put me in jail you like, I still tell Indian boys—*you no go.*'

"Then I send out men to call big camp fire meeting at Mono Lake. Then I get up on log and talk to them in own language, tell them of all wrongs done to Indians. Tell old people not let boys go to fight for this Government, tell boys not to go. Some old men answer, 'John, some boys *want* to go, we no can keep them here.' Then I tell them, if Piute boys go to war to help whites fight then I no more Captain of Piute Tribe of Mono Indians. I no more call red men together. I just John.

"Next day Sheriff from Bridgeport, called Dolan, and other men come over to Mono Lake to talk to me. I tell them same thing. Sheriff ask me not to raise trouble now, and I say, 'My people must do what *I say,* no do what white man tell them, or I no more Captain.' Well, Indian boys go all same, so now *I John—just John.*"

He folded his arms and seemed to be looking far away for some minutes. Then he silently walked out of our house and we never saw him again.

Shortly after this, we moved to San Francisco for a few years, but our interests were still in Bodie. On coming back to Bodie one spring, we heard that Captain John was very ill with pneumonia and that all the Indians of Mono Basin had gathered at his camp and were holding wierd dances and lamentations, the medicine men taking turns at chanting to the moon. Shortly afterwards, we heard that John had died.

There were the usual cry dances that lasted three days, at which no white man was supposed to be present, during which time all the effects of the deceased were burned in the usual Piute custom. John's remains were probably taken at night to some high mountain peak and rocks placed around him.

Some weeks later, my husband and I decided to make another trip to John's old home. (This time in an automobile instead of a buggy.)

Everything was in ruins. There were evidences of things having been burned every place. The iron rims of the wagon wheels and other metal parts of the wagon were lying on the ground.

Captain John's mortar and pestle

In the distance, not too far away, we could see vultures hovering over the remains of two dead animals.

As we walked away, we saw in the sagebrush a broken stone pestle and mortar.

Reverently, we picked them up and placed them in our car.

Could this broken stone bowl be symbolic of the broken heart of a once brave Indian Chief—and the pestle the white man's dagger?

CHAPTER TWELVE

The Lost Cement Mines

And The Gold Flashed Out From The Red Cement,
Till It Dazzled The Prospectors' Eyes

The Lost Cement Mine of Mono County has caused hope, anticipation, and then disappointment to many hundred of prospectors, each year, who have tried to find this rich red ledge from 1862 up to the present time.

The story goes thus—

In the Spring of 1861, a Doctor Randall of San Francisco came to Monoville. He had some samples of red cement ore in which gleamed particles of gold as large as grains of wheat, and which was worth $200 a pound. It had been given to him by a consumptive in San Francisco, whom he had treated.

The sick man, knowing he would never be able to go back to the spot himself, and being grateful to the Doctor whom he was unable to pay, had given him the ore samples and a map. The map was vague but the landmark, by which the Doctor was to be guided was Pumice Mountain (now Mammoth Mountain) in the Mammoth region.

The sick man and his brother had crossed the mountains with great hardship, at the head waters of the San Joaquin in 1857. One day they came upon this ledge in Pumice Flat, now said to be several miles north of Mammoth Canyon. Only one brother, the consumptive, thought enough of the "red stuff" to carry about ten pounds of it with him to San Francisco, but he was right; it was gold, real gold that lay encrusted in the hard, red stuff.

Dr. Randall hired men to go with him from Monoville to the Mammoth region and he located a quarter section of land near what became known as Whiteman's Camp.

The following year Dr. Randall came back and employed Gin Whiteman as foreman and about a dozen men to further help him in the search.

By this time, great excitement was rife, as many reliable people had seen the rock, and prospectors were combing the Mammoth country in search of the treasure. Among them was Mark Twain and his partner Cal Higbie of Aurora, as told in "Roughing It," but they were only two of the many hundreds all over the country who tried to find this fabulous, rich ledge. (Let me state here there are *still* those who are trying to find it.)

Whiteman's name later became more identified with the search than Dr. Randall's. Whiteman took as a partner one Van Horn. The story is told that Van Horn and a German actually *did* find the ledge but covered it up until such time as they could get Whiteman and his locations out of the way, which time never came. Whiteman, a disappointed old man, died years later in poverty, broken in health by his many years of hardship and exposure to the elements in his quest to find the red cement ledge.

It was believed by many that the Piute Indians of the Mammoth region knew the location of the cement mine, as considerable grain gold was brought into Benton by them in the early days.

As late as February, 1959, a current magazine, True West, carried a lengthy article about The Lost Cement Mine.

CONVICT LAKE

Convict Lake lies in a precipitous canyon in the high Sierra above Long Valley.

It derived its name from the part it played in 1871 when six convicts went into hiding there after a prison break of 29 hardened criminals from the Nevada State Penitentiary in Carson City.

On their way up to the Lake the convicts met, murdered, and robbed William Poor, a mail carrier. A posse was formed by men from Aurora and Benton, led by Robert Morrison, a merchant of Benton. Morrison was killed in the gun battle that ensued between the convicts and the posse. (Mt Morrison, having an altitude of over

12,000 feet, was afterwards named in his honor.)

Three of the convicts were captured in Long Valley above Bishop and two were hanged, the third was returned to prison. The majority of the desperados who escaped, however, went unpunished.

It was the Author's good fortune to come upon the following article printed in the Bridgeport *Chronicle Union* on February 7, 1903, under the following heading:

"AURORA"
By J. T. W.

"Aurora is a town of history, around whose ruins dwells many a tale of interest and life.

The wealth of Aurora was discovered in Aug. 1860 by Jas. M. Braly, J. M. Cory, and E. R. Hicks, who started from "Mono Digging," prospecting toward Walker Lake. Mr. Braly, in a letter dated San Jose, April 23, 1875, gives the following description of the discovery.

" 'We camped near the race track (a grassy flat at the head of Willow Gulch) Aug. 21, 1860, late in the evening, having left Cory's Peak that morning. Next morning, we moved camp to where the brewery now stands (a secluded spot at the head of Esmeralda Gulch); finding good grass and water, we stopped for the purpose of resting a day or two.

" 'After turning our animals loose, I went over the hill across the main Esmeralda lode, and found the first silver ore discovered on the Winnemucca ledge, at a point where we subsequently set the center stake of our claim on that lode.

" 'The next ore was found by Mr. Cory, the same afternoon, near the south end of the croppings on the Esmeralda lode.

" 'This we considered the most important prospect, for a mine, after finding ore in some veins of minor importance, we posted notices of location on four claims, the 25th of August: The Esmeralda, Winnemucca, Cape and LaPlata, and then went to Monoville for supplies and returned about the last of the month, about fifteen men accompanying us, then we organized the district, adopting mining laws and elected a Recorder. Then the trouble commenced.'

"A town called "Esmeralda" was staked off at the original site (the brewery site) but the drift of discovery North soon resulted in centering the population at the junction of the three ravines created by Silver,

"The name of "Esmeralda" was a pet one with Mr. Cory, and was

obtained from Victor Hugo's novel entitled 'The Hunchback of Notre Dame.' The Esmeralda excitement was a wild dance of death or disappointment to thousands; any piece of paper having the word printed
Middle and Last Chance hills, where Aurora grew into prominence.
on it commanding high figures for a year or two, and being as valueless, comparatively, as Confederate scrip by the Spring of 1865.

"No particular excitement was occasioned until the Fall and Winter of '62-3. The first mill was erected in the Spring of 1861 by Edmund Green. It was located in the ravine, just below the rich claims on Last Chance Hill. Mr. Green was Superintendent of the Wide West, and speaks of the ore chamber as wide enough to turn a wagon and horses in.

"By the Spring of 1864, no less than seventeen quartz mills were erected in the district, ten of them being in operation.

"In 1868, the Union mill in Aurora was torn to pieces simply for the purpose of securing the large quantity of rich Amalgam wasted around the battery and pans, so reckless and extravagant had things been carried on in early days. Doubtless several millions of dollars floated off down the creek toward East Walker river, rock that would not mill $75, a ton was cast aside.

"At one time Aurora had a population estimated at from six to ten thousand, containing many substantial and well built brick buildings, with two daily and one tri-weekly newspapers.

"Aurora has had its ups and downs, as have had many flourishing camps of today and though it is now nearly deserted, inhabited by only a few old timers, whose faith has never waned, its day of regeneration is swiftly approaching, when the hum and bustle, of business, the roar of the mills, and the steady stream of gold will prove that Aurora is truely the 'Rising light of the morn.'"

J. T. W.

AURORA—PART ONE

It is said that Cory and Braly left Aurora with $30,000 each and invested the money in prune orchards in the Santa Clara Valley.

Hicks, a part Cherokee Indian, who went back to Arkansas was said to have left the camp with only $10,000.

The first dwellings in Aurora were either tents or dugouts in the hill or stone cabins poorly constructed, having only one room and nearly always no windows.

Those early gold seekers suffered many hardships from the severe winter climate and deep snows. The altitude was around 7,400 feet.

Pine Street, Aurora

The water was generally frozen in the miners cabins as wood fires soon burned out.

When it was discovered that Aurora had the necessary, and not only that, but excellent material for making brick, four brick yards were quickly started. Lumber dropped from $350.00 per thousand to $100.00 per thousand but the price of lots jumped from $500 to $2,500 and Aurora grew in population, as a city of brick sprung up.

Flour sold at 22c per pound. Sugar at 50c per pound. All commodities were proportionately high.

People kept flocking in and new locations were made every day. From September 1, 1860, to October 25, 1860, 357 locations had been recorded.

A brick school house to accommodate Aurora's 80 school children was soon constructed. Many large two-story buildings were built on Pine Street, the principal thoroughfare.

Aurora had all the marks of permanency but Mother Nature had, it seems, favored the miners of that day by depositing most of her riches on or near the top of the ground. Several millions were taken out of the Johnson and Pond chambers.

Aurora, Nevada showing Mono County's first Courthouse

Mono County, California, then the County seat, leased, with an option to buy, the best building in town as a Courthouse. A dispute soon arose as to the boundary line between California and Nevada. The Mono County officers took up their offices in the new building, but on a rental basis only.

The result of the survey then being taken between the two States was a much mooted and hotly disputed question in the saloons in Aurora. Many Aurorans looked forward with anticipation to this County election, where perhaps all the offices now held would be declared open for a new set of officers.

Before the survey was finished, elections were held in two places, one for the Mono County set of officers and one for the Nevadans. Many voted in both places. Dissention and fighting grew strong.

When the result of the survey became known, Aurora was placed three miles inside the Nevada State line and Aurora, Mono County, California became Aurora, Esmeralda County, Nevada in 1863.

The Mono County officers soon left for adjacent places within the California boundary. Aurora, Nevada agreed to buy the Courthouse from its owners but the payments were never completed.

At this time the Civil War was at its height. Aurora, wishing to do its share in donating to the Sanitary Commission, (which would now be equivalent to our Red Cross) gave an ore specimen containing several hundred dollars worth of gold and silver to this worthy cause. It was put up at auction, the winning person again donating it to the cause. In this way it was raffled off in Aurora many times; all proceeds going to the Sanitary Fund. As Major Sherman was going east, he took the specimen with him to Boston and presented it to the Pilgrim Society of Massachusetts. In return, to show their gratitude, a fragment of The Plymouth Rock was given to him to take back to Aurora. It was placed in the wall of the Courthouse. In later years, although a systematic search was made for it, it was never found.

There were many Confederate sympathizers in Aurora during the Civil War days who were always having clashes with the Union Republicans.

When the *Esmeralda Star,* edited by Major E. A. Sherman, a staunch patriot, made its daily appearances, trouble always ensued. So high the feeling ran that at one time an attempt was made on Sherman's life, but he was only slightly wounded by the would-be assassin's bullet.

It was a well known fact that pro-Confederate meetings were being held regularly in a hillside building, and that the meetings were generally well attended.

The Union men organized two military companies known as the Esmeralda Rangers and the Hooker Rifles' Company. They met in Armory Hall and Minie muskets were distributed.

The *Esmeralda Star* of August 23, 1862 states, "On Saturday night about 11 o'clock a band of rebels made a complete pandemonium of our town and continued their hideous orgies until late on Sunday morning, cheering for Jeff Davis, Stonewall Jackson and the Southern Confederacy." The leader, A. Quinton, was arrested, placed under guard and the next morning the Hooker Rifle Company marched him to a hollow square. He was made to take the Oath of Allegiance to the Union or be sent to Fort Churchill. The Rifle Company gave three rousing cheers for the Stars and Stripes after he had completed the Oath.

An election for delegates to the Union Convention was being held in Aurora in September, 1863.

The ruffian Confederate element insisted on voting, without regard to qualification. Each bully with a gun in one hand and a ballot in the other entered the polling place and cast an already-marked ballot.

Fifty riflemen were posted outside to keep the ballot box from being stolen. The law abiding citizens had had enough grief when this trouble with the pro-Confederates ended, but the staggering climax to Aurora's trouble was not to be finished until four stark bodies had swayed in the breeze from the hangman's noose, on the hill in front of Armory Hall.

For some time, a lawless element had been rearing its ugly head around and in the outlying district of Aurora, as far as Carson City.

In December, 1861, a decent, married man named Carder had been shot in a poker game by one of these toughs for no reason except that he had been lucky at cards.

His wife had a marble headstone put over his grave. Inscribed thereon was:

"William E. Carder
Native of Tennessee
Aged 33 Years
Was assassinated in Aurora on the night
of December 10, 1861. "I will avenge"
saith the Lord
Erected by his wife Annie"

Several nights later "the ruffians" went up to the Aurora Cementery, blasted the stone full of holes, and broke it into pieces.

A gunman named John Daley seemed to have drawn around him a well-organized gang of thugs.

Stone monument on grave in cemetery, Aurora, Nevada, inscribed "William E. Carder Native of Tennessee Aged 33 Years Was assassinated in Aurora on the night of Dec. 10, 1861. I will avenge saith the Lord. Erected by his wife Annie E."

Daley hailed from Sacramento and, although only 25 years old, boasted that he had a notch in his gun handle before leaving there. In October, he killed a man in an Aurora saloon and in December

1862 ended the life of another in Carson City. His most trusted henchmen were, John McDowell, alias, "Three Fingered Jack," James Masterson ("Massy"), James Sears, and William Buckley. Many others on the outer fringe were just tools in the hands of the above named. They did their bidding as directed, among them Irish Tom Carberry, Wash Parker, Phiney Gardener, L. Vance and Italian Jim. (The last named, on being caught, turned informer).

A poor unfortunate fellow named McGuire was found dead one morning, stabbed in the back. For lack of lodging he had lain down on a billiard table and gone to sleep. A thug named Johnny Donovan, seeng him there, plunged a knife through him.

Donovan was tried before a Justice of the Peace. Although several had witnessed the killing, no one would testify for fear of reprisals, so the crime was written off the records as "justifiable homicide."

A miner was shot and killed one night when coming from work in The Wide West Mill. His body was thrown into a slimes pond where it was found some days later. A man who had seen the crime, and in fact talked to the killers, denied any knowledge of it on the stand. Verdict—"Death by unknown parties."

One of Daley's followers, James Sears, happened to be at Hoy's Station at Wellington in the Spring of 1863. He saw a horse which he fancied tied to a hitching post there. He mounted it and rode off. A German farmhand, to whom the horse belonged, was greatly disturbed and ran after him. Not being able to overtake him on foot, the German told his trouble to a Station keeper at Wellington, named W. R. Johnson. Johnson thereupon had an employee of his, John A. Rogers, follow the thief with instructions to bring the horse back.

At Sweetwater, Rogers overtook the thief, demanded the horse. A pistol fight ensued in which Sears was killed. Rogers left Sears lying by the roadside and lead the horse to Wellington.

The opinion among the right minded people was that Rogers had performed a creditable act.

Stealing a horse in those days was considered a greater crime than even killing a man. A man might be slain in the heat of passion or in self-defense, but stealing a horse was a deliberate, cold blooded, premeditated affair that left its owner stranded. Being known as a horse thief was the worst reputation a man could have.

The wrath of the thugs seemed to have been aroused against W. R. Johnson, the Station Keeper, who had sent Rogers out, rather than against Rogers; so Johnston's fate was sealed.

Several months later Johnston received a letter offering him a much better job than he had if he would come to Adobe Meadows. The first night's stop had to be Aurora. Adobe Meadows was forty or fifty miles beyond Aurora to the southeast. Johnston walked into the leading saloon which was crowded per usual. Daley and his gang filled no small part of it. Johnston drank with them but was tipped off by a friend not to go to Adobe Meadows as the gang intended to "get" him. He told Daley he had changed his mind about going and would return home the next day. They grew suspicious that some one in their crowd had "squealed" on them, so they decided to get Johnston that night.

After he had gone to bed, one of Daley's "Lieutenants" called on him and took him forcibly back to the saloon where he was plied with liquor. He tried to return to his lodgings whereupon Daley knocked him down and shot him. William Buckley drew a knife across his throat. He was then dragged into the open where "Three Fingered Jack" and "Massy" set fire to his clothes.

When news of this crime spread like wild fire through a town which had become used to "a man for breakfast," every morning, it reached the culmination of endurance.

Thug against thug *could* be tolerated, but when numerous crimes were openly committed against good, law abiding citizens, it was time for the decent element to act.

A call was sent out for a meeting and four hundred men enrolled in "The Citizens Protective Committee," organized for the purpose of helping the officers in their duties.

The Johnston funeral was held in Aurora on the following Wednesday and was the largest funeral of any ever held in the camp.

The Coroner's Jury completed its report Thursday after having heard evidence from citizens who were no longer afraid to testify.

Daley, Buckley, McDowell and Masterson were held guilty as

principals, and Wash Parker, Phiney Gardener, L. Vance, and others as accessories.

Arrests began to be made as soon as the report was finished. It wasn't long before the jail was full. Many of those of shady character lost no time in getting away from Aurora. Most of these were overtaken and brought back; but Buckley, who had headed south alone, was pursued by a possee under Deputy Sheriff Teal. On reaching Mono Lake, they divided into two groups, one going along the east shore of the Lake, the other going west. At Lee Vining's cabin on Rush Creek the possee of four men were told by the miners living there that they had not seen Buckley. A dog started to bark at something moving in the brush and they leveled their guns at the spot.

Thereupon Buckley rose up, held his arms in the air and said, "Boys you have got me this time." He was nearly dead from cold, hunger, and exposure. When being brought back, he declared hanging could be no worse than the hardships he had suffered while trying to escape.

When all four thugs had been jailed, they were given a preliminary hearing before a Justice of the Peace and all were held for trial.

The Citizens Protective Committee, fearing a delay, took over. Daley, Buckley, Masterson, and McDowell were sentenced to be hanged and the others of the gang run out of town.

A scaffold was erected on the hill in front of Armory Hall. The public were admonished to stay away but several hundred attended the executions.

A guard of The Protective Citizens Committee marched to the jail at noon, February 9, 1864, and took out the condemned men. Their eyes were bandaged, their hands tied. They were marched up the hill and onto the scaffold. Buckley addressed the crowd. He had refused the liquor that had been offered to him and spoke calmly, saying—"I deserve to be punished and I die a brave man. Adieu boys, I wish you all well."

Daley made one final request as he was led from the jail and that was for all the brandy he could drink. This was plentifully supplied. When he staggered to receive the hangeman's noose he was cursing loudly and using obscene language.

Masterson said only—"I am innocent." He was sober and cool, and it seemed his lips moved as if in prayer.

McDowell, like Daley, was under the influence of liquor and loudly and wildly protested his innocence. He pulled his hands loose, drew a derringer from his bosom, which some friend had sneaked to him, but the cap failed to go off when he pulled the trigger. He threw it down with an oath as the hangman's rope tightened around his neck.

A small cannon signaled each time the trap was sprung; and an hour and a half from the first signal, the fourth cannon shot told the tense, awaiting town that the horror and suspense of this gruesome scene was over; that the men who had terrorized the community were no more.

The four bodies swung in a light breeze until after dark, when they were cut down by friends of the dead men.

An aftermath of the Aurora hangings culminated four years later when L. Vance was shot and killed by Irish Tom Carberry in a gun fight in an Austin, Nevada saloon. Both had escaped being hanged in Aurora by only one vote.

Aurora had its bad men and its good men. Stories are written, and will always *be* written, about the gunmen and the desperados of the early West, while the names of the good sink into oblivion.

Among the latter I beg to chronicle a few of the outstanding names among the thousands of good law abiding citizens who lived in Aurora.

E. W. McKinstry, a lawyer who afterwards sat on the Supreme Court bench in California.

Horace Marden, a pioneer who was prominent in the lumber business in Big Meadows (Bridgeport).

R. R. Colcord, afterwards Governor of Nevada.

Judge F. T. Bechtel.

George L. Albright whose family name is still prominent in Inyo County and Mono Counties.

Joseph Wassen, Assemblyman from Inyo-Mono Counties.

Mark Twain's cabin in Aurora

W. M. Seawell, Attorney at Law.

Dr. C. F. Collins.

E. L. H. Gardiner, Abstractor.

And last but not least, Samuel L. Clemens, who was to achieve world wide fame under the pseudonym of "Mark Twain."

While Sam Clemens was in Aurora, he did little else but sit in one of the saloons by a warm fire, chair tilted back, his feet on the stove, keeping all who sat around him convulsed with laughter by his witticisms and stories. He and his partner, Cal Higbie, lived in a little cabin on upper Pine Street.

In one of his best known books, "Roughing It," Twain tells how he and Higbie were potentially rich for ten days when Higbie surreptitiously found and located a ledge near the Wide West; of the air castles they built in spending their anticipated wealth; of how they lost the claim as each one left it to the other to do the required location work and neither of them did it. This claim turned out to be the "Johnson Chamber" from which millions were afterwards taken.

"Roughing It" by Mark Twain is inscribed "to Calvin H. Higbie of California. A honest man. A genial Comrade, and a steadfast friend.

This book is inscribed by the author in memory of the curious time when we two were millionaires for ten days."

Sam Clemens wrote a few articles for the *Esmeralda Star* when he was in Aurora, but it was not until he wrote for the Virginia City *Enterprise* under the name of Josh that his articles really began to attract attention.

Aurora stayed in the "boom" stage for only four years from 1860 to 1864. The population during that time has been placed at 4,000 to 6,000.

There was never a general exodus, but a slow decrease in population as one claim after another failed in production.

The "high grade" seems to have been all on top, like the cream on a cake.

A shaft was sunk on the Del Monte claim in 1878 to a depth of 500 feet, but after the largest pump available failed to handle the water, work was abandoned.

Bodie about this time was beginning to show signs of becoming a real producer and many miners turned their attention to that camp only twelve miles away.

The production of Aurora has been placed conservatively at $16,000,000.

CHAPTER THIRTEEN

The Final Chapter of Aurora

In 1913, J. S. Cain and associates, Senator J. P. Woodbury, Alex J. McCone, and H. M. Gorham sold their mining interests in Aurora to Jesse Knight of Provo, Utah for $200,000.

No sooner had news of this sale been noised about, than Aurora became the Mecca for all those who wanted to get into business "on the ground floor."

The old town was suddenly awakened from its long slumber by traffic in its streets, the tooting of auto horns, the din of hammering and sawing, the noises of shelves and fixtures being pulled in and out of buildings, and the sight of deals being made on note books by men standing on the streets.

Doors and windows were being replaced in brick buildings where cavernous openings had been (brick and wood have no affinity for each other and soon part company).

The sign *"Saloon"* began to be put up and to appear on many buildings. It is not hard to start up *this* business, just a counter and a few glasses and bottles of liquor.

A little fellow named Jack Glazier, who had an Indian girl for a wife, began building at the end of lower main street a big saloon for a "Red Light District". There was a long row of brothels and the denizens of the night life moved in from all points.

Jesse Knight, who was a good living member of the Mormon Church hadn't anticipated a town like Aurora was showing signs of becoming. He worried about it. Finally his mind was made up.

The new forty stamp mill costing more than $500,000 and milling 500 tons a day, was planned at first to be constructed near town on Last Chance Hill. Instead, Jesse decided to have it built a mile from town over the hill to the north.

Jesse Knight's mill in Aurora

On a large acreage of ground not far from the mill he had fifty model new white cottages built for his employees, with cement side walks, lawns, a swimming pool, and a tennis court, but nothing in the nature of a business building.

This new town was *Mangum*, so the white sign said that hung over it, but officially it was still Aurora, as the post office had been established there ana a post-master appointed.

The post office was installed in a large brick building that had, in early Aurora, been a general merchandise store known as "The Emporium" and, in 1862, owned by Levy and Company.

Its only openings were huge iron doors in front. As they were thrown open for the first time in almost half a century, the big iron hinges rasped and squeaked so they could be heard all over town, as if announcing "Aurora is really coming back to life."

The musty, moth-eaten stock that had lain so long in the store was pulled into the light—miners clothes, long handled red underwear, stays and nursing corsets, high buttoned shoes, derby hats, stiff bow ties, bolts of black crepe and roller toweling, buggy whips, a child's crib, and at lest twenty fine black broadcloth Prince Albert dress suits marked $65.00 each. (These were sold for $1.00 a suit later to the Indians and Chinese. They actually wore them at all times, not being particular as to how they fit. It seemed Aurora had regained something of its old time affluence.)

Hanging down overhead from the beams in the ceiling were miners lanterns, milking pails, lunch buckets, cooking utensils, oil cans, water buckets, tea kettles, in fact anything that had a handle and would hang.

In the cement basement was a fine stock of liquors that hadn't deteriorated any by having aged; barrels and barrels of fine whiskey, champagne in the original straw wrappings, brandies, wines, cordials, etc. The liquor stock being worth all that the present owner had paid for the lot, building, and contents.

The Courthouse was remodeled as a hotel called "The Esmeralda." The new Aurorans said a person could go from the cradle to the grave without ever going out of The Esmeralda. The upstairs had bedrooms and a few rooms for offices, one for the Justice of the Peace. The downstairs a dining room and bar; the end room a jail intact with cells, etc., and the basement was an undertaking parlor.

The IOOF Lodge Hall was repaired, the school house again in use, and the people were living in the comfortable, repaired brick houses.

There were two miners' boarding houses, three stores, a drug store, two butcher shops, three lodging houses, three restaurants (one a Chinese), six saloons, a Chinese Laundry, all going full blast. The 4th of July celebration in 1914 was a grand event. Many Indians came to live on the outskirts. The Chinese either ran laundries or did placer mining in the gulches.

As Jesse Knight had foreseen, there *was* drinking, card playing and gambling; girls from the Red Light District in the saloons at night, trying by standing on the bars, to kick out the electric lights hung on cords from the ceiling; there *were* Chinese dens where, probably, opium *was* smoked; there was an orderly Red Light District; but, unlike early Aurora, there were no gunmen, killings, or hangings. It was an average Nevada mining camp of the 20th Century.

Aurora ran thus for about two years, but there were whispered rumors that the mines were not paying; then one morning the town woke up to hear the mines had new ownership.

Three old-timers who stayed—Andy Anderson, Gus Peterson, and Fred Walker

It was told around, without verification, that Jesse Knight had deposited a million dollars in the Wingfield banks in Nevada. That when the banks had loaned the money out, Jesse made a call on it and, to avoid embarrassment or worse, The Goldfield Consolidated, in which George Wingfield held a large interest, had bought the Aurora mines with the surplus money in its treasury. Whether this was true or not, the Goldfield Consolidated took over and the Jesse Knight interests moved out. The "Mangum" sign disappeared from above the town over the hill.

Now the new company wasn't adverse to a little night life in Aurora, or the miners spending a little money on pleasure after they had worked hard all day. A company boarding house for the miners was built over the hill. A saloon and club house was next, where the wheels spun, the dice rolled, and the cards shuffled.

Of course the old town of Aurora suffered some from this change, but the businesses there still kept going.

It was 1917 when the final shutdown came. This latter boom had lasted four years, about as long as the time of the Aurora gold rush from 1860 to 1864.

Aurora was once again a deserted camp, except for three old timers who stayed on. They were the self appointed guardians of the camp without pay.

When they were gone, the brick thieves took over and Aurora was carried away brick by brick.

Not a building is left today except the school house on the hill.

The Courthouse was torn down and the bricks brought to Bridgeport by the owners; hence it can be said that Mono County's first Courthouse again rests on Mono's soil.

CHAPTER FOURTEEN

Bodie

A little girl in Truckee, California had heard so much of the wild mining camp of Bodie to which her parents were taking her, that it was told, on saying her prayers one night, she added "Goodbye God, I'm going to Bodie."

Jim Townsend, the Editor of the Bodie Miner Index, replied in his paper of the next issue that the little girl had been grossly misquoted, that what she really had said was:

"Good! By God, I'm going to Bodie."

"Paydirt" in Bodie was discovered in 1859 by a Dutchman named William Bodey from Poughkeepsie, New York. A few months later, he lost his life in a blizzard while trying to return to Bodie from Monoville, where he had gone for supplies.

Twenty years later, in 1879, when Bodie was a rip roaring camp, a subscription was taken up to place a monument over the grave of its discoverer, William Bodey.

Five hundred dollars was subscribed for this purpose. The monument was hewn of Bodie granite with an urn on top.

Before the inscription was placed on it, President Garfield was assassinated. Public opinion is fickle, and the Masonic Lodge being strong in Bodie, it was decided to have the monument dedicated to our martyred President, and it was so inscribed.

William Bodey's grave went unmarked until recently when the E. Clampus Vitus, an organization of prominent mining men of California, had a marker put over his resting place.

The spelling of the name Bodey to Bodie was made for the sake of euphony, and pronunciation, which was further helped by Bob Howland, a stable man in Aurora putting up a sign marked "Bodie Stables."

From the day William Bodey dismounted his horse in 1859 and

The Garfield Monument, originally intended for William Bodey, Bodie

found the first handful of "pay dirt," it took nearly 20 years before Bodie was a "rip roaring mining camp."

The Standard Mine, which eventually produced millions, had a hard and varied career before it began to pour out the yellow metal to such an extent that one of the biggest gold rushes started that the West has ever known. The Standard was located under the name of The Bunker Hill Mine, the original locaters selling out their interests for twenty thousand dollars to an actor named James Stark and a jeweler named John W. Tucker.

Stark owned an opera house in San Jose, and had the idea he could use it in his new venture in Bodie. But the job of transporting it to the latter place, and transforming acoustics built for Patti into frame work for a quartz mill was a sad experience for Actor Stark and Jeweler Tucker. They ran out of money and were forced to sell their "Opera House Mill" as it was called. A Geologist Professor J. D. Whitney gave a good report on the property, and new capital was brought in. A new consolidation of claims took place. Leland Stanford, then Governor of California, was elected President, and Judge F.

T. Bechtel, Secretary. The new company was called "The Bodie Bluff Consolidated Mining Company," and was incorporated for over a million dollars.

Governor Stanford brought a mining expert up with him to Bodie. The "expert," in looking over the property advised Stanford to get out, saying he himself would not give five hundred dollars for the whole district. (The fact was that there were millions just beneath the place where they were then standing.)

The Governor took his advice and decided to abandon this seemingly worthless mining ground. The so-called "expert" lived to regret the day he gave this advice.

This put a crimp in the camp for a time. The property then passed into the hands of four men who were without money, but who had faith and brawn. Their names were Essington, Lockberg, Mooney, and Walker. The two latter soon dropped out and the Swedes Essington and Lockberg went in together.

They were boarding with a man named William O'Hara, an Irishman by name and African by birth. He grub-staked them and proved himself to be the proverbial "Nigger in the Wood Pile."

After they owed O'Hara nine hundred and fifty dollars they offered to give him the claim for what they owed. This was agreeable to O'Hara and the miners left. In vain, the colored gentleman offered the claim to any one who would pay him his nine hundred and fifty dollars. He had no takers.

Essington and Lockberg drifted around for some time and not finding anything as promising as Bodie they came back.

O'Hara was willing to let them try again "on tick" and they again began digging and hoping. Lady Luck this time decided to smile on them from a dark cave in the earth.

Timber was scarce, so they used hardly enough for self protection. One day there was a rumble and roar, their tunnel had caved. Disheartened, they went to see the extent of the damages and *there it was*, the ledge they had *dreamed* of, had *worked* for, and had *hoped* to find.

They laughed, hugged each other and shouted, until they could be heard to their own native Sweden.

It wasn't long before they had cleaned up $37,000 from their "Aladdins Cave" in the gulch. They were using an arastra and did not want to risk building a mill with this money.

When four San Francisco capitalists, Seth Cook, Dan Cook, John Boyd, and William Lent, offered them $67,500 in cash for the claim, they sold.

The new owners erected a twenty stamp mill on the property and changed the name of the claim now known as Bunker Hill to The Standard Consolidated Company. (These new owners took out the enormous sum of $6,396,270.) As the tiny buckets moved incessantly up and down the hill they san a song of *"Gold" "Gold" "Gold"* which was heard around the world, and the rush for Bodie was on.

They came from the nearby camp of Aurora, from Virginia City, which was now on the decline, from the Mother Lode, from the "City by the Golden Gate," from all points of the compass, spurred on by the tales of fabulous riches to be found on the top of the world —in the new mining camp of Bodie.

Soon there was a population of Ten thousand and the main street was two miles long.

In 1881 The Standard Mine paid to its stock holders $975,000 in dividends.

Stock in The Bodie Mining Company rose from 50c a share to $54.00 when the Fortuna Ledge was discovered, (the fabulous rich ledge that faulted and was never picked up again). Gold was so plentiful that there followed a few of the wildest, maddest years the West has ever known.

The sky was the limit in gambling, drinking, and killing. Quarrels in the saloons were frequent. It wasn't long before Bodie was called "Shooters Town."

The Red Light District on Virgin Alley and Maiden Lane was running wide open with its Rosa May, Beautiful Doll, Emma Goldsmith, Madam Mustache, and other fair ladies getting rich. The saloons were open for 24 hours.

The miners who "picked up" the high grade were free with their money.

Assayers didn't bother to assay "the stuff" first, but handed the miners about $10.00 a pound for the rock. The miners eased their conscience for putting "the stuff" in their lunch buckets by saying "Mother Nature put the gold in the ground for any body who found it."

Whiskey sold two drinks for a quarter or 10c a single drink. No man was more despised than one who drank *alone* and laid his "short bit" on the counter. He soon had the nickname of "Short Bit Bill" or "Short Bit Sam."

The time had come when gun play was not confined to the sporting element, and the respectable citizens realized something had to be done about it.

A drunken teamster named Draper beat his wife to death on the Bodie-Lundy road.

Henry Robbins was shot in Bridgeport by George Hawkins and Hawkins died in Bodie four weeks later.

Pat Reddy, the able criminal lawyer, had become the bulwark for this hardened shooting element and generally got his man off free, or with a light sentence.

"Bad Mike" a notorious underworld character stabbed a poor, harmless, half-witted fellow in cold blood. By reason of Mike's pull with the gambling element and Pat Reddy, he was sentenced to only two years in San Quentin.

The climax came when a hard working Cornish miner named John Treloar was shot in cold blood by a dapper Frenchman named Joseph DeRoche in Front of Miners' Union Hall one night when a dance was in progress.

Gossip had it that DeRoche was seen frequently at the humble home of Treloar when the latter was at work in the mine and that Treloar had frequently quarreled with his wife about the attentions of DeRoche.

There was some speculation in town as to why DeRoche had built a fine large two-story brick residence, although he was not married. (This residence was later used as a County Hospital.)

On the night of a dance, Treloar, on coming off shift from the mine, stepped into the dance hall and found his wife dancing with the Frenchman. He asked her to come home with him, whereupon

DeRoche requested that Treloar step out on the sidewalk with him and they would talk things over.

Two witnesses swore that the men had walked about sixty feet up the street and that they saw DeRoche put his hand in his back pocket, pull out a loaded gun, put it against Treloar's head and pull the trigger.

Treloar, who was unarmed, dropped a bleeding mass in the snow and died almost instantly.

DeRoche immediately engaged Pat Reddy to defend him. Pat exacted as his fee everything DeRoche owned. It was granted.

DeRoche was placed in jail, but Pat Reddy had him removed, as there was talk of lynching, and had him placed in the Bon Ton Lodging house for the night under the guard of Deputy Sheriff Farnsworth. That night DeRoche escaped. Farnsworth also left town.

When the infuriated citizens heard this, they organized the "601 Vigilante Committee."

A possee, led by the prominent business men in town, started out. At The Goat Ranch, eight miles from Bodie, they apprehended DeRoche. A vote was taken to determine whether he should be taken to the County Jail in Bridgeport or taken back to Bodie. By a majority of just one vote, it was decided that he be returned to Bodie. This sealed his fate.

When the possee arrived with DeRoche in Bodie they placed him in jail, heavily guarded, while they held a mass meeting of the "601," and took a second vote. The result of the vote was swift. By manpower alone a huge wagon crane that was used to lift the beds off of heavy wagons for repairs at Wilson Butler's blacksmith shop, was carried to the spot where the blood of Treloar still stained the snow. It was converted into a gallows.

About midnight, all arrangements being completed, DeRoche was led silently from the jail up the street to where the scaffold stood in readiness. As the noose was placed around his neck he was heard to say "Oh! My God." About twenty men took hold of the rope and, pulling on it, slowly walked away, while the body twisted and writhed in mid-air. At dawn the body was cut down and sent to the Undertaking Parlor of Charlie Kelley.

Billy Godward, the "firebug" of Bodie, aged 2½ years

When DeRoche was prepared for burial, the hangman's rope lay coiled on his chest like a snake—as a warning to other would-be-bad characters.

The lynching of DeRoche, while it had a quieting effect on the bad element of the camp, did not suppress gun play.

Five days after DeRoche was buried in "Boot Hill" the Coroner's records show that one David Banion was killed by H. Ryan and states "A quarrel between sporting men."

Shortly afterwards Officer Roberts killed J. E. Myers in self-defense. This was quickly followed by David Mitchell being killed by James Stockdale in an opium den.

The opium dens of Chinatown played no minor roll in the killings that went on.

Bodie had the next largest Chinatown to Sacramento. Its Chinese Temple or "Joss House" was an ornate, pagoda type of building, three stories high. The bronze idol of Confucius and the furnishings of the Joss House could not be duplicated this side of China.

"The Bad Man From Bodie" was a slogan heard around the Nation in the early '80's. It originated from the fact that the "601 Vigilante Committee" ordered so many bad characters to leave town that when a person said he *came* from Bodie, he was invariably asked "Are you The Bad Man From Bodie?"

In 1881, Bodie had a spicy daily newspaper called the *Daily Free Press* and a weekly *Standard News,* both under the ownership of Osborne and Cleveland. Later the well known wit and humorist, Jim Townsend, who was quoted largely in the papers of the day, edited the Bodie Miner Index. It is authentically told that Mark Twain and Bret Harte both "borrowed" many of their witty sayings from Jim Townsend.

J. S. Cain is a name which has always been closely identified with Bodie. When a young man in 1880, he knew the thrill of having taken out, with his partner Joe Maguire, $90,000 in three months, in a lease in The Standard Mine. He lived to eventually own the Standard, most of the other mines, the town property, and The Bodie Bank. His heirs, the J. S. Cain Company, still carry on.

The camp had two disasterous fires, one in 1892, and the last one in 1932, but enough of it remains to make it, at this writing, one of the best examples of a real authentic Ghost Town to be found in the West.

The fire of 1932 ran a close parallel in its origin to the O'Leary

Main Street, Bodie

cow kicking fire in Chicago. An incorrigible youngster named Billy Godward, aged 2½ years, kicked over the table at an afternoon birthday party, due to his disappointment of jello having been served instead of ice cream. The hostess spanked him and sent him home. Finding no one there he climbed up on the kitchen stove and grabbed a box of forbidden matches. He ran to the back of a deserted building and set fire to an old mattress. The flames spread up the side wall in leaps and bounds.

His mother, some time before, had opened the gate of the little play pen that enclosed Billy (and at which he had always forcibly rebelled), saying, "Go on and go. If God takes care of the rest of the kids in Bodie, He can take care of you too." Her prayer was answered as far as Billie's safety was concerned, but it was too bad she hadn't included the town of Bodie.

If the reader is still interested in knowing more about Bodie, its characters, its life, its full history, it may be found in book form in "The Story of Bodie" as written by this same author. Then you can decide for yourself whether or not Bodie deserved and sustained its reputations for being "The most lawless, the wildest, the toughest, mining camp the West has ever known."

But, dear reader, I would not want to leave you with the impression that *all* the early inhabitants of Bodie were bad. Bodie had its many thousands of good, hard working, industrious people who experienced great hardships in coming to this high, cold, isolated region and who lived up to the traditional standard of good American family life. It is only those who did the spectacular things in the outposts of civilization that are written about today.

We can say with Shakespeare:

"The evil that men do lives after them

The good is often interred with their bones"

And so it is that "The Bad Man From Bodie" still carries his guns and his bowie knives down through history in the chronicles of the wild exciting life of "The Gold Rush Days."

Index